To David
You are awesome!

Awesome

Bright Side

Building Your Bright Side

Building Your Bright Side

DONNA RAE SMITH

Wynwood Press®
Tarrytown, New York

Grateful acknowledgment is made for permission to include the following:

Excerpts from *The Prophet,* by Kahlil Gibran. Copyright © 1923 by Khalil Gibran and renewed 1951 by Administrations C.T.A. of Kahlil Gibran and Mary G. Gibran. Reprinted by permission of Alfred A. Knopf, Inc.

"Jack Is Afraid of Jill," from *Knots* by R. D. Laing. Copyright © 1970 by R. D. Laing. Reprinted by permission of Pantheon Books, a division of Random House, Inc.

"Flower Are Red," by Harry Chapin. Copyright © Story Songs Ltd., 1978.

"Eight Balloons," text from *A Light in the Attic,* by Shel Silverstein. Copyright © 1981 by Evil Eye Music, Inc. All selections reprinted by permission of HarperCollins Publishers.

Library of Congress Cataloging-in-Publication Data
Smith, Donna Rae.
Building your bright side / Donna Rae Smith.
p. cm.
ISBN 0-922066-67-1
1. Success—Psychological aspects. 2. Success in business.
I. Title.
BF637.S8S58 1991
158—dc20 91-9721
CIP

Published by Wynwood® Press
Tarrytown, New York
An Imprint of Gleneida Publishing Group
Printed in the United States of America
First Edition

To all of those special people
who gave me their own version of
Red Ball Jets by believing in me,
loving me, and supporting me.

D.R.S.

Contents

If your heart is a volcano how shall you expect flowers to bloom in your hand?

—Kahlil Gibran

Work is love made visible.
And if you cannot work with love but only with distaste, it is better that you should leave your work and sit at the gate of the temple and take alms of those who work with joy.

—Kahlil Gibran
from *The Prophet*

Introduction

I created Bright Side® as a response to my personal and professional devastation. Since its creation, Bright Side® programs have reached thousands of individuals by fostering energized thinking and providing barrier-breaking tools for people to use in their work environment. The results have been exciting to watch. I see people growing and changing by using Bright Side® skills both at work and at play.

Bright Side® went through a major change two years ago when I addressed the annual meeting of a division of Union Carbide, a Fortune 500 company. In the presentation immediately prior to mine, one of the managers said something that stunned me. In his address, he encouraged his team members to treat their clients as though God had sent them to serve. That man's remarks represent the very first time in a business environment that I had heard God's name used, not in vain, but in a very positive and encouraging manner.

Sometime later and after a great deal of thought, I realized that this manager had introduced me to a powerful idea for an American edge in the highly competitive global business market. He introduced me to a principle that gives continuous truth and lasting meaning to individual lives. Slowly, with great personal resistance, I realized that the Bright Side® concept had no power or truth based solely on the condition of self; but rather, that the power of transformation and change comes from the most powerful source in the world—God. It seemed to me that God (our Higher Power) and principles of truth were missing not only in my work but in the hearts, minds, and environment of working America.

Finally I knew I needed to gather the courage to share this knowledge so that God-in-vain would become shocking and that God-in-love would become the transforming power to shape the heart of the American spirit in industry.

My life has been filled with many experiences—both of suffering and of joy. Borne on those experiences is a change of spirit, a deep awareness that we are destroying and being destroyed by serving the bottom line rather than servicing God and each other.

> Be careful how you think; your life is shaped by your thoughts.
>
> Proverbs 4:23

Chapter One

Shattering Illusions

> We live in tyranny believing that cynicism and logic are superior to and more valid than positive, joyful, creative thinking.
>
> —Donna Rae Smith

The Bright Side concept came to me quite by accident. I was physically, emotionally, and spiritually at the lowest level I had ever experienced. I was alone. At that point in my life, I dreaded aloneness. I feared what I might find within. As a child from a dysfunctional family, and as an adult from the addictive behavior syndrome, I feared that all of the negative accusations and criticisms I had heard or played back in my own mind might very well be true.

I had considered myself a positive American. Somehow it all changed. Somehow it was all wrong. How could a positive person be so filled with the rage that I felt? I was consumed with anger and self-doubt. Along with many other baby boomers, I had chosen to follow what I thought to be the American way—only to discover that my American Dream was filled with bad thinking, mediocrity, false beliefs, addictive behavior, complacency, greed, apathy, and diseased attitudes. In other words, the direction of darkness. This falsehood of the American Dream was empowered by the greatest controlling force in the universe—fear. My fear was generated from childhood experiences and reinforced by education and the controlling dysfunction of addiction. It was a fear of being foolish, fear of rejection, fear of failure, fear of the unknown, fear of change, and fear of responsibility and growth.

My first glimpse of the codependency, dysfunctional thinking, and addictive behavior in my life was in the early 1980s. Until that time I pretended to have a perfect life, a perfect career, and a perfect family, when in fact I was from a family that hid alcoholism, from a marriage that perpetuated destructive habits of codependency, and from a business that was motivated by tactics of intimidation and adversarial relationships.

I began to see the American system as not working for me or many others. That realization was crystallized in 1981 by a striking chain of events. It was through pain and the end of denial and blaming others that my life was transformed. This was not by choice. The events were thrust upon me.

In 1981, Ohio was the machine tool capital of the world. I was in the machine tool industry and it was the first major industry in Ohio to be hit hard by the international competitor, Japan. The American machine tool giants had been manufacturing the same machines year after year. Prices increased. Delivery times lengthened. Yet, features remained the same—even the lackluster appearance of the equipment—painting them the same machine tool gray or machine tool green. The American perception, at least in the machine tool industry, was a perception of superiority. Our country, based on freedom of the individual and known for fostering individuality, was producing industries comfortable with doing things the same way—locking out change, flexibility, and innovation.

I was continuing the cycle by not rocking the boat, by not generating new ideas, by not really hearing the needs of my customers, by not thinking, by not caring for my business associates. That is, until I experienced the devastation triggered by Japan's creative approach to machine tools.

I heard that the Japanese were stealing everything from America—from ideas to technology. I discovered this was an American myth. By traveling to Japan in 1981 to tour the manufacturing facilities of Nakamura-Tome and Toshiba, I discovered:

- the YES attitude in Japanese caring—replacing the sterile American concept of service. I experienced the Japanese listening to my needs and saying YES in order to provide what I desired.
- creativity and innovation. The Japanese machine tools had new and different designs, features, and colors. This was definitely a result of the YES attitude which encourages change by finding innovative solutions.
- the Japanese encouraging their workers to be flexible, creative, open, optimistic—almost to the point of urging them to release the child from within. This was done through exercises, songs, cheers, even prayer or meditation.

What I saw in Japan caused me great concern. I began to think that the devastation in the American machine tool industry could mark the beginning of greater competition and change in many other American industries as well.

I thought, how unfair. I entered machine tool sales with one purpose in mind: money. When that industry began to crumple, I crumpled. I had no soul. I had no spirit. I had no purpose. I had spent my most precious gift, time, following false beliefs. When everything collapsed, I discovered that I was living a lie. I didn't know who I was. I realized that money could never be God or replace an inner sense of purpose and happiness. I was angered into physical illness. Finally, it was a physical ailment—a facial skin disorder—that shattered me. I could not look at myself in the mirror. Whenever I did I was reminded of my deep inner pain and conflict. My face became the outer symbol for what was wrong with my life. I came to realize that God had brought me to my knees to make me understand the profound importance of the mind and spirit.

I was filled with rage. This rage was completely wrapped with a shield of self-denial and fear which kept me from making any change. I had learned this fear from my family. It was reinforced by schools and practiced consciously and unconsciously by our corporate culture. Control by fear keeps everyone in line. These lines become barriers locking out new ideas, creativity, imagination, innovation, enthusiasm, health, spirit, and God. These perceived lines are the Great American Restraint, disguised as American superiority. This is the prison that protects the status quo.

In the machine tool industry, I learned lessons of ruthless competition: leading by intimidation and fear, and yet never taking total responsibility. It is much easier to blame or to attack. In this mode, denial is so great that the true self is buried under the guise of looking good. Not once did it cross my mind that there were other methods of leadership, or that I could personally bring about change. Whenever I suggested change, my ideas were rejected.

I felt deflated, as though small holes were being pierced into balloons, draining me of my creative energy. I recall being told that logic was superior to intuition. Creative ideas were scoffed at because they came from people who knew little about financial statements. But the financial statements were showing that money was being lost. The only solutions being offered, and followed, were those of cutting back on expenses and staff or selling harder and more. The concept of trying another way was yet to be discovered. My suggestion of providing a more inclusive warranty service for the machines was met with "it's too costly" and "we've never done it that way" rather than the YES attitude of "let's find another way." Meanwhile, the Japanese listened to the needs of America.

This kind of limited thinking begins in kindergarten when we are each given the same picture to color. "Stay within the lines" we are told. That is how we internalize the concept of conforming, of being the same. It is too risky to show the individual differences from our creative minds. So we stay within the lines of the coloring page, not trusting our own ideas.

Our culture subtly encourages our young and America's workers not to be risk-takers, to be content as followers, to not rock the boat. In fact, what is needed are risk-takers, with imaginations to increase innovation and productivity.

From success to devastation in the machine tool industry, in marriage, in physical health and appearance, I reached my personal bottom. I worked for money. The money was gone. I married for security. The security was gone. I lived for appearances. The appearances were gone. I was living in a deep, dark hole. It is the journey of finding a way out of the deep, dark hole that inspired the Bright Side concept.

When I discovered that I was an empty shell, filled with darkness, I discovered God. It was in darkness that I experienced the divine. I wonder how God or our individual spirit can be so lacking in the corporate community when our country is founded on the freedom given to us not by man but by God.

It is not easy to break through years of barriers, fear, and erroneous beliefs. How can we release the best and most promising of what exists within each individual? I discovered a key. It is to rediscover past creative, resourceful states and experiences, particularly from early childhood, before families and educators locked us into one-mode thinking.

In my pain, or because of my pain, I knew change would occur. I was silent, estranged, lonely. I was going to take action. But how could I change and take action when all that I knew was the following and gathering of information? Then I found a way, a way to transform pain into positive energy that has great application for participative management. Because I discovered "fear is useless; what is needed is trust."

One evening, alone in my bedroom at home I began to contemplate. Everything was still and quiet. Quite by accident, and with nowhere else to go, I began to review my life as though it were a movie, frame by frame, life experience by life experience. Each frame represented a single life experience remembered fully. Initially frightened by what I might uncover, I experienced the moods and emotions of each memory and made a decision as to what I would do with each one.

I experienced the negative feelings and then let them go either by burning out the frame or by diminishing and thereby completely reducing the image and the impact. How simple, I thought to myself. The positive past experiences, which were hard to find, were made powerful by enlarging them. These positive experiences were visually enhanced by increasing the size, the intensity, and the brilliance of color! By the end of the evening, I ended up with a movie of my Bright Side! I felt totally engulfed in love, goodness, hope, joy, and optimism. Without really knowing, I had the experience of being filled with God, a power much greater than the human power—a power that released my human spirit.

That contemplation was the first key to unlocking the prison that held captive the creative spirit God has given to me, the resourceful brilliance that exists within all of us. I realized that addiction, erroneous beliefs, and dysfunction were strangling

America on a national and international level, when two events occurred simultaneously. Japan's success in the machine tool industry in America coincided with my ending the personal addictions of smoking and a toxic marriage. Japan was successful because America had become complacent and was stuck in the false belief of American Superiority. I similarly was stuck in the smoking habit because of false beliefs of health, success, and happiness perpetuated by the tobacco industry's glamorous advertisements: bad thinking about cigarettes, bad thinking about American superiority, and bad thinking about love.

Bad thinking stunts growth. It is negativity in its most devious mode: it strangles new ideas, discourages change, builds a prison around the creative spirit and human mind.

This negative thinking is contagious. It reminds me of gardening. One day my mother telephoned. The beautiful plants that she had nurtured all summer were diseased. She said that new plants had recently been added to her magnificent garden. Now the new plants were diseased as well. An unhealthy condition had spread rapidly throughout her entire garden. This is how bad thinking works. It strangles healthy minds. Curing this condition requires more than adding a few healthy thoughts. As with the garden, the diseased condition will overpower and contaminate whatever is thriving and healthy.

Diseased attitudes, thinking, emotions, and memories need to be completely removed to make room for healthy growth of the creative mind. Bad thinking needs to be completely eliminated. That is what the Bright Side® process is all about.

Chapter Two

Gardening the Mind

> To accomplish great things, we must not only act, but also dream, not only plan, but also believe.
>
> —Anatole France

My childhood was not particularly joyful. Yet I remembered some very wonderful, joy-filled experiences as I reviewed the film of my young life. I had a humble beginning, growing up in Disco, Michigan. As a child, I spent a lot of time in the heart of Disco—in the country beer garden. I ate pistachios, drank Faygo red pop, and sometimes danced with my aunt Joy and my sister Debby. One hot summer day, as we drove past the beer gardens, an imaginative idea surfaced in my five-year-old mind. I thought to myself, if farmers can have beer gardens, I can have a pop garden. When we arrived home I collected every empty Faygo red pop bottle I could find. I found a number of empty beer bottles and brought all of them to my backyard.

I spent the day digging up the backyard. I planted every empty Faygo red pop bottle and every empty beer bottle. I put water in my watering can and watered the garden. Such optimism I felt about my garden. The next morning, filled with excitement and enthusiasm, I ran out to the garden to see what I had! Knowing that it took a summer for a garden to grow, I watered my garden each and every day . . . waiting for the pop garden to magically sprout. That joyful memory from my childhood taught me precious lessons for my adulthood.

- There's no such thing as a mistake. We learn lessons. (My greatest personal success and growth have been from the lessons of "mistakes.")
- How wonderful it is being five. When we are five we know how to have fun. We know how to play.
- We are all highly creative at age five. Creativity is not reserved for the "genius," but rather we each are highly creative in our own individual areas of genius.

In every human being there is a talented, gifted individual filled with genius, and a child's wonderful enthusiasm. The American challenge is to free that child and to rediscover individual giftedness and national greatness. Japanese corporations encourage their people to be like five-year-olds in order to cultivate the creativity, optimism, genius, openness, freedom, and flexibility that exists within the child in all of us.

Imagine for a moment the sense of joy, love, resiliency, adventure, and curiosity of a six-month-old. Begin to consider what happens when that child is guided not by encouragement and a sense of adventure but by discouraging remarks like "No, you'll fall."

I spoke at a national meeting with the famous American sociologist Ashley Montagu. Much to my amazement, Montagu presented a film of a child learning to stand, crawling to explore the environment. The child was utterly joyful, curious, experimental, open, playful, and sensitive. Montagu said that we are all designed to be like the child—to grow in those childlike potentialities in love, work, and play—to grow as if to live and to love are one.

When I teach the essence of Bright Side, I present a vision of an exciting adventure that blends individual purpose with corporate vision, universal meaning, and childlike potentiality. It is human productivity at its highest, supported by encouraging independent thinking, individual differences, creativity, spirituality, and deep caring.

My pop garden is still planted in Disco. Whenever my children and I are in Michigan, they insist on visiting my pop garden. It's still hidden, never having grown. But it symbolizes what *has* grown—my own childlike potential and spirit—so that today I am able to give you tools for releasing your creative five-year-old and your childlike potential.

The Bright Side gardening tools are simple, fun, easily remembered, and easily used. The Bright Side results are often powerful and lasting. Bright Side works. Bright Side doesn't mix health and disease. Bright Side begins in a fresh new place, on a brand-new street, releasing and expanding the best that exists within you. Here is how to

☆ *GARDEN YOUR MIND* ☆

Create an Emptying Page and a Filling Page. On the Emptying Page write with pencil very lightly "LET GO!" On the Filling Page write "ENERGIZE!" with large letters using brilliant colored crayons or markers. On the "LET GO!" page, empty out negative or limiting thoughts, memories, experiences, feelings. Now fill the "ENERGIZE!" page with empowering and positive thoughts, feelings, memories, experiences. Be certain to visually minimize the negative and visually enlarge the positive with brilliant color.

• *Emptying*

Title your Emptying Page. Write lightly in pencil, "LET GO!"

You may want to begin with letting go of the critical, doubting self that caused the lines of restraint that we learned as children. Make the words, images, or pictures light and small. Empty out the ideas and thinking that are the bars of your personal barriers.

LET GO OF SELF-DISCOURAGEMENT!

• *Filling*

Title your Filling Page. Write in color, "ENERGIZE!"

You may want to begin by filling with your encouraging self or by recalling a joyful experience. Make the words, images, or pictures large and colorful. Release your childlike potential. There are no lines here!

FILL WITH SELF-ENCOURAGEMENT!

Chapter Three

Red Ball Jets

> Always remember to forget what made you sad, but never forget to remember the things that made you glad.
>
> —Elbert Hubbard

For me, the early 1980s was a time of genuine pain and despair. I was floundering due to a lack of purpose. I had busily followed the precepts established in the machine tool industry, only to discover that the Japanese had overtaken us in our own home market. Japanese excellence in quality, short lead times, and better pricing began to seriously erode the ailing U.S. machine tool industry.

I started in the machine tool industry as a sales executive. I then became a manager/officer in a family business. When the machine tool industry began to tumble, so did I. I wondered, What is my purpose? Who am I? Am I using my talents for the betterment of others, or am I blindly following a path of not thinking about or caring for the people I serve? I saw a vast difference between the Japanese product and the American product. I felt unclear about my role in perpetuating a system that did not encourage thinking or change. Certainly, I was a product of an industry that justified the status quo and labeled it ''excellence.'' Many of us were blind to the part we played. Never did I consider what I could do to make a better product or better world. I was more interested in material gain, even if it came at the expense of my clients or co-workers. Nor did I feel empowered to suggest change.

Then I met Allison Roe.

Allison Roe, a native of New Zealand, set the 1981 women's record for the twelfth New York City Marathon. Business, future marathons, and training brought her to Cleveland. It was an unusual opportunity for me to meet her, and even more unusual that she would be my house guest while she was in Cleveland. A friend had introduced us, thinking that knowing Allison would be good for me. I felt a real surge of excitement. It was the first excitement I had felt in a very long time. Never had I had the privilege of being that close to a world-class champion.

I was immediately impressed by Allison. Very warm and friendly, she was genuinely interested in sharing her knowledge and experience with me. I instinctively knew she was a role model of excellence.

The contrast between the two of us was stark. She bubbled confidence, zest, joy, and hope. I was depressed.

But Allison Roe lit a fire inside of me. I felt almost lifeless when she entered my life, but she gave me invaluable training tools that transformed me, erasing my dark way of thinking. Her presence in my life became the spark that ignited the Bright Side concept.

As she began to talk about marathon training, I knew the time had arrived for me to accelerate my learning curve. I had invited my friends who were runners and athletes to meet Allsion. Much to my surprise, what we learned went far beyond sports. When Allison described how she trained for a marathon, she focused on mind training almost exclusively. I began to cling to her every word. She flatly stated that 90 percent of winning in anything was mind, a positive mental attitude. In other words, believing that you can.

I could feel myself rejecting what she said. I thought, if she is a winner because she is positive, then that makes me responsible for my junk thinking. Yet, I had every reason to be negative and depressed . . . look at what the Japanese had done to us! (It certainly was not *my* fault, and it certainly had nothing to do with *my* thinking.)

Allison disclosed her mind-training formula. First, be positive. Second, mentally and positively picture the event. Third, in the mental picture, see yourself and the detail. In her case, the detail included the exact course of the marathon and her specific competition down to the clothing she would be wearing. Fourth, accompany the positive mental picture with positive self-talk. Fifth, combine the positive mental picture with a positve mood state, with emotion. She concluded that her positive mood state was that of winning, total confidence, success.

As she described these steps, I could feel an unwrapping of deep awareness and insight. A memory that I had completely repressed came whirling out of my mind. It was a memory of an experience I had had as a five-year-old child living in Disco, Michigan.

The big event in Disco was the fair. Like most fairs, ours had amusement rides, pie-baking contests, cake-decorating contests, watermelon-eating contests, and races. I was interested in the race for boys and girls in grade school, so I went to my mother and I told her that I wanted to enter. She and I went to the big city of Utica to get a pair of Red Ball Jets. I believed that anybody who had those magic shoes could run faster and jump higher than anybody else. The minute we got those running shoes, I put them on, and my mother and I began to practice for this race. Wearing my Red Ball Jets, we went out to a dusty country road. She rode a bicycle as I ran.

Every day we would practice. My mother would encourage me, saying things like, "Donna, you are fast!" And I remember thinking, of course I'm fast, I've got Red Ball Jets! Then she would say, "Donna, are you a strong runner!" I would look down at my feet and I would say, yes, of course I'm a strong runner, I've got Red Ball Jets! And my mother would say, "Donna, you are going to win that race!" And I looked down at those Red Ball Jets and I thought to myself, yes, of course I can, I've got Red Ball Jets! We practiced for that race every day. I was using mental picturing without even knowing it.

The day of the race came. All seventy-five young participants lined up on the starting line. I looked down at my feet and I saw those Red Ball Jets. Then I had enough courage to look at the children to my right and to my left. I was the only one with Red Ball Jets! It was at that moment that I said to myself, I'm the winner! I knew in my heart and in my mind that I was going to win that race. That was the only thought in my mind.

I looked straight ahead at the starting line, focused on winning, focused on being the first person to reach the finish line. The starting person said, "Get on your mark, get set, go!" Off we went! Each of us ran as fast as we could, but there was only one person who took first place that day. It was me.

That winning experience had been totally forgotten because it had been buried under negative, critical thinking, the garbage thinking of my adulthood.

As I recall that experience of victory as a five-year-old, I now realize that it would have been just as powerful had I taken second or third place. The experience taught me valuable lessons. Above all, it taught me to believe my ideas: the idea that I could run a race, and the idea that I could win.

Frequently in my seminars, people ask me if I am telling the truth about this experience. Let me assure you that I am. Yes, there were children who were stronger and taller and faster. But the biggest difference between me and those other children that day was that I believed. I believed not in reality, but in potential. And I believed in the fact that I could win the race. That was the only thought that went through my mind—winning. And, of course I believed in the magic of Red Ball Jets.

Today I believe in much more powerful, deeper kinds of things. What happened to the magic of believing in ourselves, our potential, our goodness, our ability? How is it that those beliefs have faded?

In Bright Side seminars, I ask people to rediscover a past positive, to think back, preferably to their childhood, to a time when they felt successful, when they felt like winners. Sometimes, because so many Americans come from families that are considered dysfunctional, it's difficult for a person to recall a positive, encouraging experience from childhood. So I encourage them to find a positive experience from any period in their life, because each and every one of us has had at least one good thing happen. We have had at least one experience of really feeling successful, of really feeling like a winner.

How often we imprison and anchor ourselves by recalling just negative past experiences!

What I would like you to do now is rediscover a "past positive." Think back in your own life to a time when you had success. It can be any kind of success, like climbing a tree and being able to get right back down, riding your bicycle, getting a good grade on a test, passing driver's education, or being selected for a team. Then think about how you felt.

As I recall my Red Ball Jets experience, I feel exuberant. I feel the same sense of accomplishemnt that I did when I was five years old. I feel personally empowered, even though that experience happened over thirty years ago.

Chapter Four

Rediscovery

> I am more involved in unlearning than learning. I'm having to unlearn all the garbage that people have laid on me.
>
> —Leo Buscaglia

For many years, my happiness was determined by the outside world and my outer self. My behavior was dictated by expectations and models presented by the media and reinforced by American culture. I had no individual identity, no sense of personal mission. I believed that the more material possessions I could acquire, the happier I would be. I was absolutely frightened by the prospect of inner discovery, not realizing that it meant finding what was already there—my true self.

The same outside-inside philosophy has brought corporate America to near ruin, as experienced in fierce global competition and serious financial challenges. It began with the emphasis on the bottom line and Wall Street, quashing individual talent in the rush for buyouts, mergers, and acquisitions.

For individuals and companies to be effective and creative, there has to be a transformation that begins deep inside. The book *Happiness Is an Inside Job* by Jesuit psychologist John Powell addressed this issue. With companies searching for ways to increase productivity, and individuals searching for happiness and meaning, it is vital to break out of the outer habits of destruction and to teach inner habits that will bring lasting joy and serenity. This will eventually result in higher creativity, productivity, quality, and service to industry. I like to compare it to the inner housing of a machine tool.

A parallel in the machine tool industry would be that of differentiating between a machine overhaul and the remanufacturing of a machine tool. A machine overhaul used rubber bands, bubble gum, glue, and bandages to temporarily make a machine run. It was a stopgap measure. On the other hand, rebuilding a machine brought the machine down to the bare casting so there could be substantial change. Much like the inner essence of machine tools, the individual person needs to be polished at his or her innermost core in order to be revitalized and rejuvenated. This innermost core is the spirit.

The outer image of a machine couldn't influence quality production any more than how-to skills of selling, time management, and management development can influence the mental and creative energies of individuals.

Dr. Nche Zama, surgeon at The Cleveland Clinic, surgically removes organs from the newly dead to give new life to the living. He can never go physically into the deepest essence of the human mind, or reach the spirit that embodies each individual. Yet, symbolically, when we go deep within to reach our own heart and spirit we give new life to ourselves, our family, our companies. "The key to all life is the spirit within," says Jack Kahl, CEO of Manco, Inc., a manufacturer/producer of Duck Brand tape.

Throughout my childhood, I heard negative, limited, destructive talk that told me I had little value or worth. It began in nonspectacular ways. Well-meaning yet insensitive people would say to me:

"You think too much." "That's a crazy idea." "You whine."

Such comments were later reinforced by an education system that instilled fear for lack of perfection; by a family system and culture that created a deeply embedded sense of shame for the alcoholism, abuse, and divorce that existed in my family. Then I married a man who preyed on my sense of insecurity. My positive mental path had not been frequently traveled. It was overgrown with weeds from disuse. I had more often used the negative mental path, creating deep grooves and ruts that were easy to follow and fall into.

Yet, when I learned to recall a past positive, I felt so personally empowered! It felt so different from the imprisonment caused by the negative mental path. I began to understand that my direct and indirect experiences influenced my thinking and behavior.

For Joseph Turgeon, CEO of Zaclon (formerly a Du Pont division), the concept of rediscovering past positives had an important application to his team's performance. When I first presented the Bright Side concepts to his management team, Zaclon was approaching its second-year anniversary since its buyout from Du Pont. Zaclon was in a very economically challenging period. Any idea of celebrating its second year was restrained by serious financial considerations.

After introducing this concept of rediscovering a personal past positive, Joe Turgeon came up with a team application that brought great positive energy and vision to his team. Zaclon had celebrated its first year in business with a party. Remembering the Zaclon balloons, napkins, and banners brought feelings of success to everyone. The memory of a first anniversary's celebration and a successful first year were also buried in the minds of his team members. He wanted to create the good feelings of success in the same way that I had taught his team members to rediscover their own "Red Ball Jets" experience whenever they needed to feel exuberant, confident, or energized.

Quite inexpensively, he celebrated Zaclon's second year: he recelebrated Zaclon's first year by re-creating that year's anniversary party. He and Jim Krimmel, president of Zaclon, hung the banners and balloons and other success symbols.

None of this was communicated in advance to his team members. They walked into the team conference room expecting a standard monthly team meeting. In its place, they discovered a team "past positive" that generated powerful I-can-do-it feelings.

This is success building on success. It is a stimulating approach to breaking through mental barriers and to creating an energized sense of optimism and creativity. When we rekindle a past experience, we believe in it again today and in the future.

THE REDISCOVERY PROCESS

This may be challenging on first attempt. However, as with any new habit, the more practice and repetition, the more permanent it becomes. Former Cleveland Brown's football star Jim Houston compares this mental and physical practice to his football experience.

First, we gather information. Then we put the information into action, interaction, and repetition. The learning then becomes a part of us.

This same process applies to the building of positive energy, positive individuals, positive relationships, and positive teams. Practice rediscovery of past positives, then believe it, apply it, and practice it.

Steps

- Think back to your childhood to any positive experience, perhaps that of climbing a tree or riding a bicycle for the first time.

- If you feel you can't recall a positive experience from your childhood, then proceed to another time in your life. Perhaps you got a good grade or were selected as a team player in some activity or sport.
- As you think about this past positive experience, give it detail. Where were you? What did you do or say? What were you wearing? What about the description of the other people around you? What happened? How did you feel?
- Use positive, encouraging words in the present tense. The mind cannot differentiate between what is real and what is imagined.
- Begin to draw a mental picture image or symbol of this past positive experience to anchor the memory and associated positive feelings.
- We are all artists, creative . . . so release your inner child and, using color, begin to draw a bright, colorful picture, image, or symbol of this past positive experience.
- Now add an encouraging and positive written description. Use present tense as though it's today's reality.
- Bring to mind your positive mood state.
- Anchor-in the remembrance with a red ball, label, or sticker, symbolizing your own Red Ball Jets.
- Give the experience a positive title. Give yourself a positive nickname and describe your energy level and mood state.

☆ *BRIGHT SIDE ENERGIZERS* ☆

• *Rediscover a Past Positive*

Positive Title	Red Ball Jets Because I wore Red Ball Jets and won a race when I was five.
Positive Nickname	Do-it-Donna I matched the D from Donna to the D of Do-It.
Positive Mood State	Exuberant, totally energized, a "10."

• *Rediscover Your Past Positive*

Individual or Team Past Positive Experience

↕

Positive Title

Positive Nickname

Positive Mood

Energy Level	1 nonenergized	5 so/so	10 energized

Chapter Five

The Adventure

Life is a daring adventure or nothing.

—Helen Keller

When you get to the end of your rope, tie a knot and hang on.

—Franklin D. Roosevelt

My daughter, Maressa, rushed into our house, beaming with excitement. She had returned from a fifth-grade camping trip and was full of enthusiasm. She informed me that she had experienced the most exciting event of her life.

I immediately stopped what I was doing, curious to know what could produce such excitement in a ten-year-old. Before I had time to ask, Maressa rapidly began talking. She explained that the children had explored caves. Some of the caves were bear caves! As she talked, I shivered, picturing the dark cave environments that I had once explored and remembering only the fear I had felt. Maressa's sense of adventure heightened as she began to describe the caves. She was thrilled to tell me that those caves were so tiny and narrow that they could accommodate only the small bodies of children! The adults, much too large, had to remain at the cave entrance while the children went on this adventure alone.

Maressa explained that the fifth-graders lined up at the mouth of the cave. There was one flashlight, held by the front child. The children would have to enter in single file, holding one another's hand, passing on, from front to back, information about how and where to move.

Just as the children were about to enter one cave, a well-meaning adult asked for a show of hands from the children who thought they might not finish and might want to come back early. After all, the cave was narrow, and it would be easier for the children to return if they were at the back of the line.

The question immediately piqued my interest. My attention heightened as I became more interested in the children's responses, and how it would influence the outcome. Maressa said a few of the children did raise their hands. I asked Maressa if her hand went up! Incredulous, she told me no. She continued to reconfirm that this was indeed the most exciting, thrilling experience of her life.

The cave, she explained, was dark and narrow, with ankle-deep water in certain places. She described in detail exactly how she and the other children moved in this narrow passage. Her pitch heightened as she told me she got stuck at a very narrow point, not fully hearing the directions from the child in front of her. She told me that she screamed and tried maneuvering to free herself—but to no avail. I fired the questions: Did you think about returning? Did you turn back? She laughed. She said it never crossed her mind to return. Maybe her sense of adventure gave her the necessary energy, but she was able to free herself as easily as she had lodged herself in this narrow passage. She beamed with pride. Her energy and spirit fostered encouragement at such risk-taking.

Then I remembered the children who weren't so positive about this adventure. "Maressa," I asked, "what happened to those children who thought they might return early? Did they?"

Maressa paused and gave a thoughtful look. "Yes," she replied.

"All of them?"

She again paused to think, and once again answered yes.

"What about the others?" I inquired. "Did any of the other children return early?"

After another thoughtful pause, she answered no.

What an example of how our mental picture influences human behavior! A suggestion of doubt had produced fear in some children and stifled their sense of adventure. As a result, they were afraid to take the risk.

Adventure, that empowering sense that moved Maressa to the most exciting experience of her life, is the component that American industry needs to cultivate in the nineties. A sense of adventure propels us, frees us. It keeps us on a path of light, not darkness. It is the adventure of Bright Side: life, energy, fearlessness, vitality, courage, emotion, love, trust and creativity. It is risk-taking, not only physically but mentally, too.

As we face today's highly competitive global market, with serious financial considerations and a vital need for creativity and enhanced productivity, it is the nontangible mental energies that will make competitive differences and bring a sense of purpose and meaning to the individual as well.

Individual rejuvenation requires the removal of barriers to free our sense of adventure—that same sense of adventure found in ten-year-old children who explore caves. "I assure you, unless you change and become like little children, you will not enter the kingdom of God." (Matthew 18:3)

When conversing with my friend and client Nancy Vetrone, president of the Inc. 500 Company, Original Copy Centers, she credited two qualities with making a difference in her company's success: enthusiasm and caring. She believed that if every one of her people possessed enthusiasm, Original Copy Centers would continue growing in success. She described nontangible qualities that cannot be seen but make a difference in the success of her highly profitable organization.

There aren't any shortcuts. The role of a manager has changed at the end of this century with the very nature of work itself. It is becoming less physical and more cognitive . . . less material and more spiritual. It requires you to assist your people in solidifying their sense of self-esteem. The art of leadership is to stimulate employees to think creatively, to learn, to share, to cooperate, and most importantly, to understand. I'd call this genuine management by involvement.

Consider this Chinese proverb as presented in a Progressive Insurance Company seminar: "Tell Me—I'll Forget, Show Me—I May Remember, Involve Me—I'll Understand." Employee empowerment feeds on this understanding and involvement process.

Most people believe that fear impairs their job performance daily. I contend that fear can be unlearned. In Bright Side, I use five keys to launch an Adventure of Spirit. This is the adventure where we encourage participants to see change as a normal part of life, and to realize that the work environment can become a safe place for self-expression and creative freedom to discover new ways.

We suggest continually seeking out "bright ideas"—even if they come from another industry or country. We encourage reward and recognition for the big and small wins and changes. We encourage respecting all people for what they know, for what they can learn and for what they want to do and be. We believe that no one has all the answers. We set the stage for adventure and discovery by sparking human curiosity and spontaneity. There is no better time than now to commit. Best described by Goethe, commitment begins when we feel empowered, experiencing freely who we are and what we love to do.

> Until one is committed, there is hesitancy,
> the chance to draw back,
> always ineffectiveness.

Concerning all acts of initiative and creation,
there is one elementary truth
the ignorance of which kills countless ideas
and endless plans:

That the moment one definitely commits oneself, then
providence moves too.

All sorts of things occur to help one
that would never otherwise have occurred.

A whole stream of events issues from the decision,
raising in one's favor all manner of unforeseen
incidents and meetings and material assistance,
which no man could have dreamed would come his way.

Whatever you can do or dream you can,
begin it.

Boldness has genius, power, and magic in it.

Begin it now.

—Goethe

THE FIVE KEYS

Key #1 Novel Tools
Key #2 Playful and Positive Interactive Experiences
Key #3 Rediscovery and Expansion of Past Positives
Key #4 Mental Picturing of Future Positives
Key #5 Trust for the Inner Sense of Right Direction

Novel Tools

Novel tools are simple toys (stars, bubbles, stickers, clay, crayons, etc.) that engage our creative mind and access our emotions. They build a simple, easily remembered, positive image. They are concrete. They are tools that are used simply, daily, to break out of old negative behavior patterns, to get us thinking in new ways.

The tools are energizing and renewing because they bring uplifting pictures to mind. They remind us that we create our own moods and states of motivation. They also activate positive memories from the past. The tools slap our senses like cold water being splashed on our body, breaking stress and tension. They stimulate and improve our brain function.

Playful and Positive Interactive Experiences

Learning is reinforced by active participation. The five stages of learning are impact, repetition, utilization, internalization, and reinforcement.

Interaction (the actual experience) internalizes learning, making it a part of us and our experiences. To intellectually and rationally understand adventure is vastly different from actively participating in an adventure. Active participation heightens our mood state and "we know" what adventure is and does. We buy in to that understanding not because we have gathered the facts, but rather because we have experienced it. Our experience with the associated personal changes in our emotions and energy makes it valid.

As we view the children exploring the caves, we see that their joy, experimentation, and enthusiasm propelled them to a desired outcome. The results are increased team participation, increased creative thoughts, and heightened mental energy—a true sense of spirit and fun.

Rediscovery and Expansion of Past Positives

Accessing our positive mental file is often more difficult than accessing the negative mental file. Most of us have had more experience with the latter. Although we believe we are positive and encouraging people, we may have limiting thinking habits.

According to John Bradshaw, author of *Homecoming: Reclaiming and Championing Your Inner Child,* we have recorded twenty-five thousand hours of critical parenting scripts which we play back in adulthood. Our positive mental file is rusty and sometimes difficult to reach. With the aid of Bright Side's playful and positive interactive approach and Bright Side's novel tools, we can more easily bypass the years of negative patterns and rediscover one success or encouraging experience, and use that success to build on more success. To the extent that we admit a past experience to be true, we believe it of ourselves today.

Mental Picturing of Future Positives

Human behavior is determined by our mind, our mood state, and our physiology. Mental picturing of joyful and desired outcomes influences our behavior, even if we're fantasizing. Our every thought has a biochemical correlation that influences all the cells in our body. Research shows that peak performers in business and sports are very skilled at mental picturing and combining that mental picture with a resourceful mood state.

Trust for the Inner Self of Right Direction

This is our intuition. It never seems to make sense, yet when we trust it, it works. This aspect of human nature is not proven by logic but is the source of our discoveries . . . about ourselves, our world, and our work.

When we begin to hear and trust the quiet inner sense of direction, we begin to feel a core of truth and love, confirming our own inner core of love, value, and truth. This inner discovery gives us the courage and impetus to do creative work and to love, even in the workplace.

☆ *BRIGHT SIDE ENERGIZERS* ☆

To create the sense of adventure, to free yourself from the bad habits preventing you from reaching your inner core, to become totally energized for the adventure of spirit, select one of these Bright Side energizers. They will prepare you for peak performance. Remember, motion changes our emotion.

- Shake your arms, legs, and body very playfully to shake off stress.
- Pretend that the negative thinking is a monster on your back, so now whip off that monster.
- Do jumping jacks.
- Hug yourself. Hug others.
- Give a shoulder and neck rub to yourself or to others.

It is helpful to record your energy level before and after the energizers. A "10" is very exuberant, confident, and creative, open to change and adventure. A "1" is when you are nonenergized, negative, tired, or tense. A "5" is "so-so."

I promise participants that at the end of a Bright Side session, they will feel totally energized, even when feeling like a "1" or "2" at the start. Typically, energy, confidence, and creativity are increased after completing two or three of the energizers described above. It is absolutely exhilarating to see a group become exuberant, open to change and challenge, filling with greater confidence and trust.

At an IBM/Bright Side meeting managers were called upon to provide creative solutions for their customers. Their positive and open attitude toward change was clearly exhibited in their creative and alive response to the Bright Side energizers. These energizers gave IBM participants an opportunity to stretch their thinking (along with their bodies) and to challenge old traditions and try new ideas. They discovered, as do many other Bright Side participants, that the energizers not only create physical exuberance, but also instill heightened mental and creative energy.

After you have recorded your beginning and ending energy levels, you are ready to continue the Adventure of Spirit.

> All I have seen teaches me to trust the creator for all I have not seen.
>
> —Emerson

Chapter Six

Barriers: What Are They?

Don't find fault, find a remedy.
—Henry Ford

As I conduct seminars across the country, I ask Bright Side participants to evaluate the barriers to positive performance potential from two perspectives: one that has personal significance, and one that limits their team or organization. It is less threatening to select a team barrier. Not surprisingly, though, the individual and team barriers are often the same.

Although the initial strategy is to identify barriers, ultimately a barrier is transformed into a desired outcome: transforming a problem into an opportunity. Without doubt the overarching barrier to full performance is

FEAR

There are all types of fear: fear of failure, fear of appearing foolish, fear of the unknown, fear of making mistakes, fear of change, and fear of self.

Fear knows no professional category. Fear knows no age. Fear inhibits CEOs, machine operators, children, secretaries, parents, teachers.

The number one fear as identified in barriers is fear of failure. This occurs when we do less, or settle for less, to avoid shame, humiliation, or pain.

> I want to say something to this person but the fear comes: I'd better not (he may misunderstand, he may be in a hurry, etc., etc.). These fears are not based on the present situation, they are based on the past, and I don't have to be governed by what once went wrong. The two of us are standing here in the present. What is the situation now?
>
> —Hugh Prather

Fear is the opposite of trust. Fear has a dance all its own, as depicted in the poem "Knots" by R. D. Laing.

Jack is afraid of Jill
Jill is afraid of Jack

Jack is more afraid of Jill
   if Jack thinks
   that Jill thinks
that Jack is afraid of Jill

Jill is more afraid of Jack
   if Jill thinks
   that Jack thinks
that Jill is afraid of Jack

Since Jack is afraid
   that Jill will think that
      Jack is afraid
   Jack pretends that
      Jack is not afraid of Jill
So that Jill will be more afraid of Jack

and since Jill is afraid
  that Jack will think that
    Jill is afraid
  Jill pretends that
    Jill is not afraid of Jack

Jack tries to make Jill afraid
  by not being afraid of Jill
and Jill tries to make Jack afraid
  by not being afraid of Jack

The more Jack is afraid of Jill
  the more frightened is Jack that
    Jill will think
      that Jack is afraid

etc., etc.

As that poem illustrates, fear freezes us, physically and mentally. According to family counselor Virginia Satir, "When your body feels tight, your brain often freezes right along with your tight body, and so your thinking becomes limited as well." One of my associates was so overcome by fear of failure and humiliation that he was unable to leave his home.

For most of us, those feelings of fear and humiliation are so frightening that we cope by denial. How often do we actually set ourselves up for being, doing, loving, or living less so that we are not disappointed, shamed, or pained? I believe that is how we got the expression "no pain, no gain."

I recall being paralyzed by fear when the machine tool industry in America collapsed. I felt vulnerable, like a crab having molted its hard shell. My entire identity was a professional mask. Once that collapsed, I was afraid of discovering my true identity. I feared that the real me couldn't possibly be acceptable or worthy. I feared that I had no value without the identity of my work. My livelihood and identity were threatened.

I remember being on the shore of Chesapeake Bay, allowing waves and sand to sweep over my feet. With no motion or movement by me, suddenly I was trapped by the tide, paralyzed by inertia.

That is what fear does to us.

Yet fear can also propel us to greatness. My friend and client Jack Kahl, the CEO of Manco, the manufacturer/producer of Duck Brand tape, concludes that we are only truly living when we have the feeling of being out on thin ice. And he concludes, "I'm glad on this ice."

He believes that the fear faced by corporate leaders is masked by their pretending they are in charge. This protects a leader's image of power, money, and control. Kahl believes leaders must role model both risk and willingness to change. This cannot be accomplished by any other person in a corporation, yet he estimated that fewer than 5 percent of corporate leaders are willing to change, learn, and grow. "There is more lip service than action, keeping the group in authority in control of others. The greatest learning disability is the human wiring. It is the software inside that is the barrier." This protects the boss's power. Kahl says what most only think: "I'm a little kid inside. I'm scared."

Kahl surrounds himself with great teachers, high-fiber human beings. Two of his teachers are Sam Walton, the dynamic and humble chairman of Wal-Mart; and Socrates. Over Kahl's office door is a quote from Socrates that speaks eloquently to the issues he addresses. "One thing only I know, and that is that I know nothing."

Because of this quote and Jack's human wiring, everyone at Manco can freely admit they don't know everything. The boss himself admits it. Jack believes that if he wants his people to learn, and if he is to create a learning organization, he has to be the first to show his willingness to be retrained. A willingness to deprecate oneself demonstrates a person's real, internal strength versus the need for power and control. Kahl credits this idea to Sam Walton. After all, how can people feel empowered if their leader believes he is smarter than they?

As I see it, that is a championship CEO setting championship standards for other CEOs. Champions are found not only in sports, but in business as well.

Fear of Playing

This is actually fear of making fools of ourselves. We are overly serious about our work and our personal lives. It is frightening to try unusual or different things. Albert Einstein wrote about the freedom to play with concepts and ideas as a vital source of creativity. Those of us who come from dysfunctional families look at play as inappropriate, especially in serious arenas like work. Yet the ability to play, even if it appears foolish, encourages risk-taking and creative thought.

Cleveland Advanced Manufacturing Program (CAMP) was founded by Cleveland Tomorrow, a council of executive leaders from manufacturing companies. The goal of CAMP is to build regional manufacturing excellence that can compete in the global market by bringing technology advances and technology transfer to industry. CAMP works in partnership with industry, academic institutions, and government.

At one meeting to generate innovative team approaches, CAMP let its hair down. The team began to have fun and play with ideas. That sense of playfulness produced a multitude of new ideas and new relationships. As a result of Bright Side, CAMP team members now set aside personal biases to work (and have fun) together. By using the gray matter (putty), they were able to shed tension and barriers. Team members viewed one another in new ways, becoming creative and cooperative. Individuals who normally didn't contribute blossomed with creative ideas and cooperation. An overly serious critical approach would have turned off the right brain, the source of creativity and imagination, and would have maintained the status quo of distant relationships.

Fear of the Unknown

We often avoid situations and circumstances when we feel fearful or intimidated due to a lack of clarity concerning the outcome. It is very secure knowing the outcome. We are at risk when the end results are out of our control. It is safe to stay out of the dark cave. Turning around and going back to safety is more reassuring than going forward toward the unknown.

Victor Ide, the human resources manager of Roberts Express, tells it best in an experience he had in his friendship with David, who is deaf.

Victor and David met in St. Louis. Victor wanted to avoid David because David represented the unknown. Victor was also concerned about making a fool of himself by trying to communicate with this deaf man. Like many of us, Victor did not want to go forward to an unknown. He preferred to avoid this person, even though he was knowledgeable in signing because of deaf relatives.

Victor told of a time when he and friends were laughing. David wanted to understand the humor, but Victor didn't want to go through the involved effort of communicating its meaning. Victor said, ''Never mind.''

Yet Victor could see David's desire to communicate. He remembered his own mother and how often people viewed her as rude because she couldn't hear. Her lack of response, although due to a hearing problem, was perceived as snobbish.

Victor finally risked communicating with David. As a result, he grew in ways that benefited him and Roberts Express. Victor now takes advanced sign language classes and hires physically handicapped people. Most notably, he is no longer afraid to address the issue of bringing physically handicapped people into the work environment. After all, most of us, in one way or another, are handicapped, most significantly by our thinking.

LIMITED VIEW

This is an inability to see the strength in one's self or one's environment. I once read that everything we need for success is right beside us, that we do not need to travel to find the resources we need.

Earl Nightingale, whose syndicated radio series, "Our Changing World," motivated listeners nationally, tells a beautiful story of a man who, while mining for diamonds in Africa, sells his farm in search of the ultimate success. He ends his life broken and penniless, never having found a mine. Yet, on the farm he sold, there was found a great diamond mine.

That inner core, that diamond mine, is often our own inner energy and creative potential. We spend most of our time on the outside searching, when in fact the wealth of ideas and talent is smoldering within, waiting to burst into flame.

CUSTOM-BOUND

Being bound by custom is the barrier that led to the current American demise in global competitiveness.

"We've always done it this way," and "It never worked that way before" join forces with superiority, complacency, and apathy. Our thinking and behavior become rigid. We believe that what we have done in the past is still superior to any other method.

However, past methods may no longer be functional or superior. Growth, learning, and change must be ongoing, not halted by success. Success isn't the end, but rather the substance that can give rise to more or greater success. It is the ''Peak to Peek Principle'' outlined by Robert H. Schuller. Having had a peak experience, one gets a glimpse of other opportunities and future potential.

My son, Brant, having experienced his first win in swimming competition, was able to take that success and apply it to soccer, too. That fall, when the soccer season began, Brant realized that he could apply the speed from swimming to the speed of running in soccer. Parents and coaches went up to him, wondering if this was the same boy who had barely run at all in previous soccer games. Brant could have continued in his usual behavior of running slow. Instead, he chose a different response that triggered greater success. We do have a variety of responses to choose from, often ones we have yet to learn, having not learned them as children.

PAIN AVOIDANCE

It is often easier and less painful to give up when faced with so-called obstacles. We are so comfortable with what is familiar. We can predict the outcome when we stay on the familiar course. I believe it is through the discomforts that we give birth to a new level of understanding. The pain shatters the old self and the old understanding that limits our potential.

It reminds me of the scripture reference to dying unto the old self: ''I solemnly assure you, unless a grain of wheat falls to the earth and dies, it remains just a grain of wheat. But if it dies, it produces much fruit.'' (John 12:24).

I recently heard of a similar metamorphosis—of caterpillars giving way to butterflies. A caterpillar is transformed physically and biochemically by slowly emerging through the constrained opening of a cocoon. If the journey is made easy by artificially widening the opening, the caterpillar will not make the transformation into a brilliant, colorful, flying creature. It will not become a butterfly. It will not fly.

Imagination

I believe the single most important factor to reaching one's goal is the body of ideas born and nurtured in a person's imagination. We limit ourselves by not thinking, imagining, or dreaming big enough mental pictures.

Allison Roe was not born a champion marathoner, but she believed in what she created in her mind—a desire to become a world-class champion. The first creation began in her imagination. The second creation was manifested in reality accomplished through hard work. Allison opened a door to a path for me to actually "see" a dream at the end. My dream, from my imagination.

SENSORY DULLNESS

Motivation is determined by our mood state. Our mood state influences that of everyone around us. Have you noticed what happens to your energy level or your mood state around a negative, deflating thinker? In the machine tool industry, I remember taking a creative idea to a decision-maker. The response was negative, cynical, and disempowering. It felt as though a needle had punctured holes in my balloon of self-esteem. I felt de-energized.

Today, through the self-nurturing of positive internal feedback, I can more adequately persevere and be resilient. I recall the caring support and coaching of friends who believed in me before I actually believed in myself. It is the surging energy of emotional power that builds the confidence necessary for the successful undertaking of any task.

POLARIZATION

Another blind alley in the transformation of barriers today is polarization. That disunity creates opposition and tension which halts and stunts creativity, trust, and productivity.

Patti Ribble is from a small town in Washington. As a young woman she successfully completed half an Ironman. She then qualified for the Ironman Triathlon in Hawaii. It was a thrilling opportunity—except, as a college student, she couldn't afford it. However, her mother and brother believed in her potential. They encouraged the families of the town to donate so Patti could travel to Hawaii. She did compete, and although she did not set time records, the experience demonstrated what can be accomplished when people come together, focused on and cooperating toward a goal of vision.

ADDICTIONS

Addiction, according to psychotherapist and author Anne Wilson Schaef, is any process over which we are powerless. Addictions take control of us, making us do and think things that are inconsistent with our personal values. Process addictions are as damaging as substance addictions. These are greed, destructive thinking, blind focus on the bottom line. They cause people and companies to stoop to any level to complete their objectives. Addictions feed destructive thinking patterns, thereby polluting minds. It requires courage, perseverance, and confidence to break free of them.

But an amazing example of breaking free of the addictions, in the corporate sense, was accomplished by Jack Dannemiller, the current president and COO of Bearings, Inc. Prior to joining Bearings, Inc. he was president and COO of a $1.7 billion organization. A proxy fight ensued. Then the company was put up for sale. It was a battle for power, control, money—a battle of greed. A leveraged buyout was made and large debt incurred. Downsizing was necessary. Jack Dannemiller was faced with a paramount decision—whether to remain. If he remained, he would have the potential for large financial gain at the expense of not using his talent, or nurturing the talents of others. He chose to leave. Dannemiller states that the best business book he knows is the Book of Proverbs. "It provides good advice for every president."

☆ *BRIGHT SIDE ENERGIZER* ☆

Select a barrier that relates to you. Write it lightly in pencil.

____

____

____

Now "let go" of the barrier by writing in bold color a detailed positive description of your ideal desired outcome, as though it is reality. Accompany this vision with specific steps or behavior for accomplishment. Anchor this in your mind with a mental picture and meditation.

____

____

____

Chapter Seven

Tools of Wonder: Breaking the Barriers

> In playing and perhaps only in playing the child or the adult is free to be creative.
>
> —D. W. Lawrence

It was Christmas. My daughter and I went to get our Christmas magic: our tree. As we browsed and searched, none of the trees measured up to our expectations of the perfect tree. Dismayed, I wondered if this would be the Christmas without the magic of discovering the tree just for us.

A helpful man suggested we cut down our tree. Ordinarily, that kind of suggestion would be immediately dismissed. After all, I had never sawed anything, let alone held a saw in my hands. I chuckled to myself, remembering how shocked my son was when I sewed a button on his shirt. He exclaimed, "Mom, you can sew!"

But a Christmas without magic is like no Christmas at all. I made a decision. "I will cut the tree down," I announced.

Off we trudged through acres of beautiful pines, searching out the perfect one. Then we saw it, big and majestic against the bright blue sky. Satisfied, I turned my attention to the task. I could hear my negative self-talk.

I'm never going to be able to do this, I thought.

But aloud I said, "Well, let's get going."

How am I going to do this? I worried to myself. To my daughter I said, "Well, I better lie on the ground to get the right angle." (As if I knew.)

This is awful, I thought to myself. I am simply going to pretend I know what I am doing.

With each anguished thought, I could hear my daughter encourage me with nods, smiles, and words of "That's great, Mom." I knew I couldn't disappoint her or myself. I decided that even if it took me hours and hours, I would cut that tree down!

I began to saw. Nothing happened. The saw got stuck. My daughter continued to encourage me, stating that she was pulling the tree toward her—to give it a little help. Good, I thought. She hasn't caught on to how inadequate I feel. I was struck by the hope, excitement, and pure confidence in her voice that said, "Yes, Mom, can do it!"

Don't give up, I shouted to myself, keep trying. With that, I made my first cut. Maybe I can saw down a tree after all, I rejoiced. My "Yes, I think you can" thought coincided with my daughter's, "You're doing it, Mom!"

Maressa pulled harder. I worked faster. With each cut, I repeated, "Yes, I can; I am doing it," until Maressa loudly, jubilantly bellowed, "Timbeeer!"

We celebrated, dancing, laughing, and hugging. We did it! She and I! It was wonderful.

It was empowering to shatter a concept of self that had been painted by our culture and my family regarding the roles for women and men. What limiting beliefs do we need to shatter to help ourselves unlock hidden talents, use more of our resources, and realize more of our dreams? Imagine your toy chest or treasure chest filled with exercises and toys to help you access your optimism, vitality, and creativity!

These characteristics of childhood are our powerful motivators. The tools we need for access are toys of wonder. I am always amazed and moved when I see Bright Side participants move from resistance, fear, and skepticism to exuberance, creativity, openness, and trust, by using the Bright Side tools and techniques. A transformation occurs once participants begin to experience positive energy and emotion.

When I first saw people respond to the process, I knew something powerful and special was happening. When I saw the same pattern repeated with other groups, all ages, both sexes, and all socioeconomic backgrounds, I knew the ideas that I had developed for self-realization and empowerment were universal. What I have also seen is that most of us, to some degree, come from similar family and cultural roles that have wounded us.

That woundedness is reflected in everything that we do. It contaminates our relationships both at home and at work. The Bright Side tools work. As psychologist Abraham Maslow said, "If the only tool you have is a hammer, you tend to see every problem as a nail." Thus, to garden our spirits, and nurture the child within, Maslow believed that psychology dealt too much with human frailty and not enough with human strength. He looked to a more positive side of humanity. To garden our mind, cultivating that flowering child from within, we need our tools of childhood . . . the toys of wonder.

In *Build Your Brain Power: The Latest Techniques to Preserve, Restore, and Improve Your Brain's Potential,* Arthur Winter, M.D. and Ruth Winter write that the brain can be developed and repaired, to a degree, even in old age; that we can train the brain to preserve, restore, and improve intellect through selective stimulation. We use between .01 percent to 10 percent of our brain capacity. Research shows that decline in mental function is not an inevitable part of aging. It is believed that an enriching environment increases the manufacturing of brain glial cells, which provide support and aid to the neurons there.

These neurons perform the main work of the brain, processing impulses from far-flung nerves of the sense organs. Thus, the stimulating Bright Side approaches help our brain function, and keep us young and vibrant.

• *Tools of Wonder*

CRAYONS. Even smelling crayons will bring back memories and feelings of your magical young years.

Crayons shatter the routine and habit of black and white. They are a colorful reminder that we can shatter limiting beliefs and paint visions, of a new self, a new organization, or a new product.

RED BALLS AND JACKS. This childhood toy helps anchor-in and recall our own "Red Ball Jets" past positive experience. The jacks symbolize "letting go" of the negative and "filling" with the positive. The red ball itself carries the picture of this positive experience and can be easily used in a meditation included at the close of this chapter. The red ball reminds us to be resilient and to bounce back. This familiar children's game is one of the best exercises for the cerebellum. It requires hand speed and coordination. Exercise increases mood and brain functioning—we think better and feel better. It is also a reminder that repetition creates changes in our brain cells. Practice helps us learn and change.

BUBBLES. This is a "solution" that washes away years of fear and mistrust. It cleanses the mind, heart, and spirit to reveal childhood spontaneity and purity. It is a symbol for the childhood language of love, freedom, and truth. It is for bubbling our creative wonder and individuality. It is the single most important tool for personal empowerment.

"AWESOME" STICKERS. These remind us that we are wor-

thy and awesome, to start each day fresh, renewed and awesome, with the awesome cheer.

I am awesome
You are awesome
We are awesome
Yes! Yes! Yes!

The "Awesome" stickers remind us of the vital importance of positive self-talk, belief in self, and encouraging feedback. The cheer is a simple way to build energy and vitality. Here is an example of how it brings out the "champion" self.

It was my son's championship basketball game in the fourth grade. It was his first season playing basketball and he was thrilled with the prospect of being on a championship team! It was the first time *his* team in any sport had made it to the finals!

I had Awesome stickers that I use in Bright Side workshops. I wondered about taking those Awesome stickers to the players and coach. Knowing how kids sometimes feel about what their parents do, I cautiously and optimistically asked my nine-year-old what he thought about the sticker idea. He thought it was an awesome idea!

The coach thought it was an awesome idea too. He placed the stickers on himself and on all four assistant coaches. Then, he went to each player and placed an Awesome sticker on his sleeve, giving each individual a pat on the back and positive words of encouragement. The boys smiled. Their faces actually glowed. They became noticeably more relaxed—and I heard them calling each other awesome. And awesome they were! They won the championship game by over ten points to a team they had always lost to. Never underestimate the power of awesome thinking and the awesome cheer:

I am awesome
You are awesome
We are awesome
Yes! Yes! Yes!

STARS. The one novel Bright Side tool that is almost universally popular is a star. When is the last time that you received a star? If you are like most Bright Side participants, you will say that it was in kindergarten or grade school that you received a bright gold star.

Recalling that experience, you can surely feel your spirits soar. Then why has it been so many years since you have received that symbol of goodwill?

There is often tremendous fear associated with the giving or receiving of positive feedback. Even though we may talk about the virtues of being positive, most of us have learned and relearned skills of negativity. As children, we are bombarded with critical parenting, and the media further bombards us with controlling, destructive, or violent messages. The stars, because they relate to our innocent, playful, positive self, activate the healthy memories within us. These novel tools engage the Bright Side within. It is always exciting to see how exuberantly people respond when they discover that they will be receiving a packet of gold stars. They trigger the inner child, the positive self, the creative mood. The reaction is universal and felt by employees in all professional categories.

Stars are used to help trigger early memories of goodness, value, and worth; to remind us of the powerful importance of meeting psychological needs; to hold others in positive regard; to find something to respect and care for in all people—especially ourselves, and to give positive feedback ten out of ten times. When we ask for positive feedback ten times, we will often receive it no more than five or six times out of ten. However, when we ask for negative feedback, we may get it more times than what we wanted. I believe that is evidence of the active critical self we have recorded from childhood.

Often, we are even uncomfortable with giving positive feedback to self; to sharing the "self-positive" with others. We have learned that it is boastful, bragging—that it simply isn't polite to hold ourselves in such positive regard. In a sense, we have learned to keep ourselves and others out of a highly motivated or peak performance state.

Motivation is about our mood state. The mood state we are in influences the mood state of those around us. After seeing the exuberant responses of Bright Side participants while giving or receiving positive feedback coupled with using the stars, I am convinced that the cornerstone to an enhanced motivation state is verbalized positive regard for self and others.

"WHAT'S IMPORTANT IS YOU" POSTCARD. The blank side is for a personal message or for a quotation that can be used in reflection. Often, the quote we insert is "Treat a man as he is and he will remain as he is. Treat a person as he can and should be and he will become as he can and should be." (Goethe)

RED BALL STICKERS. These stickers are strategically placed on telephones, mirrors, car dashboards, and briefcases to visually remind us to recall and use our energized past positive, our own "Red Ball Jets" experience. Participants are encouraged to practice daily bringing this past positive state to mind and to use the past positive nickname whenever feeling tense, anxious, or uncertain.

This image is strengthened through meditation and visualization.

BALLOONS. They remind us of the importance of breaking through fears of foolishness or of making a mistake, when we fill the balloon and empty out and let go of the negative. Another strategy is to stand back-to-back with a partner. While back-to-back, touching each other, recall yourself as you looked in the mirror this morning. Mentally picture the silly, goofy, outrageous faces you made as you shaved, washed your face, or put on your makeup. When you are satisfied that you have selected the most outrageous facial expression or movement, mentally practice it. Then turn to your partner, giving her or him that absolutely funny expression. In doing that, you can never stay in a state of fear or mistrust! You might also try going back-to-back with a partner to mentally picture the most outrageous and positive thing you can do to your partner with the balloon. When you have practiced mentally, turn to your partner, and pass on your balloon magic!

KNEADED ERASER. We stretch, shape, and form the eraser as we generate more ideas, release ideas, and discover new solutions. Many Bright Side participants keep this "gray matter" putty on their desk or in a pocket to serve as a reminder that we can generate hundreds of alternatives or solutions to any of our life challenges.

I recall once watching a six- to nine-month-old child. What curiosity and persistence I observed! This infant had rolled into a lowered area in between cushions and pillows and was experimenting with dozens of ways to move out. Without giving up, stretching and trying many ideas, she finally discovered the solution! One Bright Side participant said gray matter reminds him that he can come up with hundreds of ideas for a solution in a five-minute span. Gray matter is also like clay, reminding us to play and be as creative as children.

PENCILS. Used for writing down the negative ideas so as to empty out the woundedness, the dark side, the critical, limiting self that exists within each of us. To eliminate garbage thinking.

THE BRIGHT SIDE HUG CARD. To remind us of the vital importance of hugging, holding, and touching, which can give life richer, greater meaning. We must take risks and touch. Hugging is almost a natural instinct. Touch facilitates trust and empathy. Infants die when deprived of touch over a time, and children can become severely depressed.

Try these ways to increase touch:

- Hug and touch people who are closest to you.
- Hold hands with your spouse, friend, or child.
- Give a pat on the back and positive recognition to someone you admire, respect, and/or like.
- Form a team huddle before beginning a meeting.
- Give high-fives, the high hand slaps most often demonstrated by athletes.

The Bright Side Recharged Card

Using each letter of the words "Bright Side" reminds us of the Bright Side tools and techniques.

Bubble. Be optimistic.
Be playful.
Bubble the exuberance of your positive, playful, and exuberant inner child.

Rediscover empowering past positive experiences.

Imagination and intuition are to be used and trusted.

Garden your heart, mind, and spirit with tools from your childhood: stars, stickers, cheers, hugs, crayons. Love, feeling, courage, resiliency, creativity, trust, a sense of adventure.

Have habits of humor, laughter, hugging, tears. Smiling and laughing are major expressions of happiness and increase blood flow and oxygen to the brain. Crying and laughter may help our body rid itself of toxic biochemicals made by stress, although Dr. Lee Berk, assistant professor, Preventative Medicine, School of Medicine, at Loma Linda University, maintains that research is still in the horse-and-buggy stage.

Trisk. Trust and risk. Increase trust by risk-taking. Trust your own ideas, thoughts, feelings. Be a risk-taker of your mental, emotional, spiritual, and creative self.

Starpower, positive regard for self and others.

Inner dialogue. Transform it to one of self-love, self-acceptance, and self-encouragement.

Dark side—learn from it and "let it go" to make room for your Bright Side.

Energize with emotion and fill with your Bright Side.

Our parish priest and author, Father John Kinkoff, concluded his Christmas seasons sermon: "We are always children."

I smiled.

His message for an eternity.

To me. To you. At home. At work. Our rich inner child knows no boundaries.

One day, I made a quick stop at the Federal Express office. A woman there had a box containing a teddy bear and chemicals used in chemotherapy. The toy and medicine were for a four-year-old child with cancer. The woman, air-expressing the medicine to Orlando, Florida, told tales of giving away bears, baseball caps, trips to Disney World. "What age kids?" I inquired. Smiling, without pausing, she said, "All age kids. Aren't we always children?"

☆ *BRIGHT SIDE ENERGIZERS* ☆

This is the toy I will use today.____________________

____

____

This is how I will use it.________________________

____

____

• *Red Ball Visualization*

Feel your mind new and fresh—ready to learn new methods, ready to shape new ideas, ready to expand beyond where you are today, to go beyond where you have been. Feel yourself ready, teachable, accepting of fresh, positive, and new perspectives. Your mind is eager to learn; eager to expand and go beyond where you have been; eager to diminish and erase barriers and obstacles to your happiness, health, or success. With a sense of newness and expectation, begin to focus on deep and relaxed breathing.

In your mind, picture the Red Ball Jets name tag from your personal rediscovery. Picture a red circle. If the red circle is a different shape or color or if you see it in another way—by hearing or seeing words—that is fine. Stay calm, relaxed, focused on your easy and peaceful breathing. This red ball or red circle is the anchor to your Bright Side. It holds the positive past experience that you rediscovered, filling you with exuberance and confidence. That experience (name it by title) is always with you in the forefront of your mind ready to be used whenever you need to be confident or energized. This red circle is within your control. You can move it, you can make it different sizes.

Now, very comfortably, move it next to your body, slowly making it larger. Now empty out into the red circle feelings, attitudes, beliefs, and experiences that are barriers to your success. Empty out feelings of fear, hurt, anger. Remove any barrier you have identified as negative. Empty and remove anything that stands in the way of your accessing your rich inner treasure—the wonderful, joyful person within.

Since the red ball is within your control, begin to move it slowly away from you—filled with negativity. As it moves farther and farther away, see it become smaller until it is a very small circle in the distance. Now empty out the negative, the barriers. Simply, "let it go." Use the gray matter to help you diminish and erase those obstacles to your potential and your abilities.

After letting go of the negative, bring the red circle back to you—filled and continuing to fill with goodness, joy, love, confidence. Image your powerful past positive and the powerful mood state of complete confidence and resourcefulness. As the circle gets closer, see it become larger and more powerful. See it filled with positive ideas, positive selves, positive feelings and expectations. See it filled with the positive past experience you rediscovered. Once the red circle has returned next to you, feel all the positive ideas, images, and feelings begin to fill your heart, mind, body, and spirit—completely energizing you with each breath as you continue to fill with extraordinary and awesome potential.

Now take one minute to fully concentrate on that which you need the most for yourself: filling with positivity; emptying barriers; mentally picturing your positive potential or your past positive rediscovery—your Bright Side.

Now find a safe place in your mind to keep the red circle to use at any time to empty the negative, to fill with the positive, or to trigger your Bright Side. Allow yourself to feel completely refreshed and renewed as though it is a beginning of a new day filled with wonderful surprises. Begin to gently open your eyes, move your feet, hands, and body and come fully to the present—feeling totally energized and absolutely awesome. That is your Bright Side at work!

Chapter Eight

Play Can Be Productive

The supreme accomplishment is to blur the line between work and play.

—Arnold Toynbee

In the ''Twilight Zone'' television series, Rod Serling produced a show, ''Kick the Can,'' in which an elderly man believed the way to become young was to act young. As fellow golden-agers moved forward on that belief and played the childhood game Kick the Can, they once again became children, young and hopeful.

The images and tools that have great power today are often those of control and violence. While traveling back to Cleveland from New York, I heard yet another radio broadcast about a person critically injured by an unknown assailant in Manhattan's most chic area. One of my AT&T Bell Labs team members, having lived in Manhattan, shared an experience about having been seriously wounded by a gang member while having dinner in Chinatown.

Tools of mergers and acquisitions, another weapon of our society, instill the same kind of deep mistrust at manipulation for the profit of a few. Just as life is changed by a critical injury from a gun, a life is changed by the weapons of buying, selling, restructuring, divesting, and merging. These weapons help snuff out the richness of each individual.

People have become very familiar, and thus very comfortable, with tools of destruction. These are familiar out of commonly learned experiences. I am always amazed when people can discuss these experiences and corresponding tools as though they are most appropriate. This is what people have learned is a normal part of being an adult.

We read in the New Testament:

> All of us fall short in many respects. If a person is without fault in speech he is a man in the fullest sense, because he can control his entire body. When we put bits into the mouths of horses to make them obey us, we guide the rest of their bodies. It is the same with ships; however large they are, and despite the fact that they are driven by fierce winds, they are directed by very small rudders on whatever course the steersman's impulse may select. The tongue is something like that. It is a small member, yet it makes great pretensions. See how tiny the spark is that sets a huge forest ablaze! The tongue is such a flame. It exists among our members as a whole universe of malice. The tongue defiles the entire body. Its flames encircle our course from birth, and its fire is kindled by hell. Every form of life, four-footed or winged, crawling or swimming, can be tamed, and has been tamed, by mankind; the tongue no man can tame. It is a restless evil, full of deadly poison.
>
> James 3:2–8

Yet it is often deemed appropriate and acceptable for people at home or at work to be verbally defensive and abusive, cursing at each other with belittling remarks or sarcastic humor. "That's a stupid idea; that's crazy; your head is so small you must have a tiny brain.'' The tongue is potentially our most destructive weapon. Working with corporations, I am shocked at how frequently people belittle and nibble away at each other.

Such behavior is so common that we are uncomfortable with the healthy tools of creativity and fun. The defensive, rejecting behavior of corporate America is accepted as normal. We have been socialized and conditioned to use, and accept, defensive behavior.

Having fun by using playful tools from our childhood can be immensely beneficial. They help us:

- Reduce stress.
- Remember positive childhood experiences.
- Reframe our current perceptions, ideas, or thoughts.
- Find a light, bright, humorous side.
- Have fun.
- Break through limiting beliefs about our potential.
- Break through barriers of fear and mistrust.
- Remember how to play.
- Remember the positive current experience.
- Create energy.
- Demonstrate the need for playfulness for creativity.
- Take ourselves out of the same old rut.
- Lift ourselves outside of our limits, boundaries, or beliefs for problem solving.
- Keep ourselves open to learning.
- Break through negatively held perceptions of self.

Working with a group of executives at AT&T/Bell Laboratories, we finished the problem-solving game of nine dots:

The participants are asked to draw only four connected straight lines to connect all nine dots, without lifting the pencil from the paper. It is only after looking outside of the nine dots that the problem is solved. Solutions that I see repeatedly:

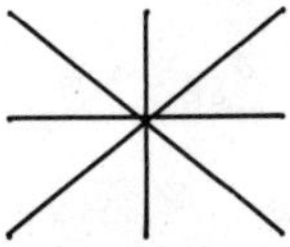

Oops! All 9 dots need to be connected.

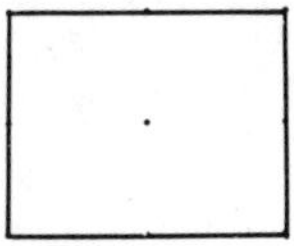

Oops! What about the middle dot?

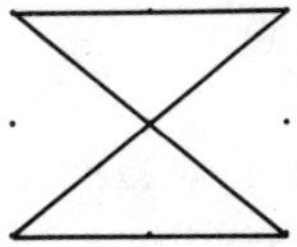

Oops! What about the side dots?

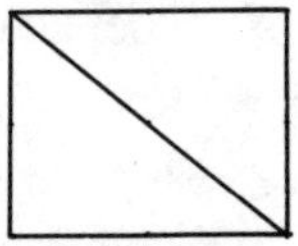

Oops! Please use only four straight and connected lines.

Over and over, participants try familiar paths of dot connecting. It is only after actually going beyond the obvious—the boundaries of the nine dots, that there is a solution, a creative insight. One solution follows.

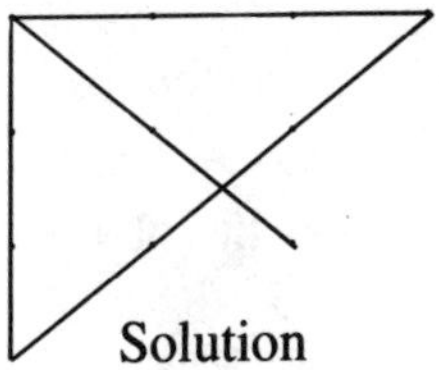

Solution

After the managers worked together as a team for nine-dot problem solving, the team leader introduced a toss game, using fruit and bottles of bubbles. The team was instructed to keep lowering the time it took to toss all items to each other in a specific pattern. The final time to accomplish this tossing game, in a consecutive pattern, was two seconds. In a lively and fun manner, the team clearly exhibited these cooperative teamwork traits:

- Trisking action
- Communication
- Interaction
- Facilitation of each other's efforts
- Utilization of each other's ideas
- Acceptance and support
- Trust
- Absence of fear of failure
- Good listening skills
- Cooperative intentions
- Absence of fear of making a mistake
- Absence of fear of foolishness
- Liking each other
- "Letting go" of the negative
- Openness and sharing of ideas
- Experimenting with new ideas
- Positive feedback and coaching

In fact, research shows that cooperative efforts result in higher productivity than interpersonal competitiveness.

Insight into how to toss the objects in two seconds, which is most easily generated when people are having fun, was preserved. Having fun encourages creativity, good relationships, and productivity.

Balloons are also great tools to introduce. Balloons represent celebration, festivities, and success. Balloons bring back childhood memories of play. At Zaclon, balloons from their successful year-end celebration are brought out to remind team members of what they can do.

Balloons can be used in a variety of toss games:

- Keep the balloon in the air.
- Keep several balloons in the air.
- Use only your head (or any other part of your body) to keep the balloon afloat.

Team members can join up with a partner, back-to-back, each with a balloon in hand, and create a playful (maybe outrageous) use of the balloon with his or her partner.

Team members can blow up a balloon, filling it with negative, limiting, or critical thoughts, ideas, and feelings. Once the balloons are blown up, all team members let go of the balloons . . . thus letting go of the negatives.

Or, similarly, team members can blow up a balloon, filling it with the negative. Once blown up, the balloon is tied. The negative is stomped out of the balloon.

Balls and jacks, another childhood game, is often introduced in ongoing Bright Side seminars. The red balls and jacks are integrated into the seminar to also lock into the memory the specific learning of the ''Red Ball Jets'' rediscovery.

The red ball represents rediscovery of a past positive, and a simple red ball mental-picturing exercise is used for weeding out the negative and feeding the positive.

Why the repetition? It is necessary. It has taken people years to get where they are today because they have repeated bad habits of behavior and thinking or because they have not learned the skills necessary for positive habits. Thus, it is necessary to learn by repetition new ideas, and to use as many tools as possible to form deep new patterns of behavior and thinking.

Often, it is difficult to connect bottom line results to the intangible energy of the human mind and spirit. But, I have seen it work. One Bright Side client, Zaclon, clearly credits the Bright Side process with improved relationships, enhanced teamwork, increased productivity and creativity. This is what Zaclon president Jim Krimmel said:

"Take our potassium silicate operation. We tried to start it up the end of September, but we had all kinds of difficulty. One of our managers has been a production-type manager for a long, long time, and is very set in his traditional management ways. He first tackled the start-up process in that manner. He sat down with his crew when he first ran into a problem and said, 'Look, you have to do this, read the book, here you have to do this, and I'll decide this.' Although he knew that was contrary to my own philosophy, he acknowledged that this is the way he thinks he had to do it. I told him to go ahead and do it. After about three days of frustration and not solving the problem, I told him the quote: 'Treat people as they are and they will remain as they are, treat them as they can be and you want them to be and they should be and they will become.'

"Following that prompting, a lot of the barriers were knocked down, drawing on some of the things that were done in Bright Side. The workers reached the consensus as to what to do, and [the manager] didn't have to dictate what had to be done. The problems disappeared. That was a very strong demonstration of the power of this thing. I am sure the manager will approach all of his future problems that way.

"The biggest problem, you know, is that in the final analysis, business is about people. It is about employees who are people, it's about customers who are people, and consultants who are people. It's about learning how to deal with people on a level playing field, regardless of their function and position.

"I am very encouraged. It really takes time, but people change because they see value in this approach. This particular operations manager grew up a great deal during this experience. You know, you hear these little things like 'all problems are disguised opportunities,' and when you are in the middle of the problem, it may not feel that way. But now I am very glad that we had this start-up problem because I think it changed the mind-set of some of the operating management people, who were skeptical of this process."

Bright Side tools are often provided as a simple method to reinforce learning and positive action. Desired behavior must be rewarded. Playful tools bring joy to the work environment. For many people, the novel gift of congratulations gives them the praise and recognition to encourage them to continue growing.

Entire companies also utilize the concept of reward and recognition with new ideas. At Manco, CEO Jack Kahl presented a challenge to his team: If they reached sales of $60 million at the end of their fiscal year, Kahl promised to swim the duck pond in front of Manco's corporate headquarters. The team reached their $60 million goal. Kahl kept his word.

The event blossomed into a celebration that featured a high school marching band and a buffet luncheon. The Manco cafeteria was filled with balloons bearing Manco colors. Despite damp, cold weather, the entire company marched out with Kahl on the designated day. He sported several bathing suits—all cleverly made just for this event. The mood and energy were high. He did swim the pond. He followed the memorable endeavor with bonus checks that were individually presented at the luncheon.

Documented acknowledgements of hard work were given to each Manco partner.

Kahl's novel approach went beyond the limits of the nine dots.

His inclusion of a bonus for the team achievement was complemented with a community gift of $50,000 to Providence House, a crisis nursery in Cleveland. Sister Hope, founder of Providence House, was present. He, Manco's leader, dared to take a risk. The entire day—swim, rewards, lunch—created an environment of exceptional energy and benevolence. Who would not want to work hard again next year?

Research shows that giving may indeed increase the body's ability to manufacture exhilarating biochemicals like endorphins.

My personal experiences of giving demonstrates this.

Prior to a Bright Side program in Toronto, Canada, I was dashing around, completing preparation for the presentation. On schedule, with not a minute to spare, I decided to stop in the hotel lobby for a morning beverage. Much to my dismay, I discovered a huge line of people. How I wanted to walk up front, get the coffee and go! My urgency was clearly recognized by a man right at the front of the line. Without my asking, he offered to let me go first! I thought, this world is a wonderful place after all. (I also wondered if I would have volunteered to do the same.) Then an idea, inspired by Good Samaritan studies, struck me. Without saying a word, I purchased coffee for that benevolent man. His giving had inspired me into giving a small gift as well. I felt good throughout the day. In fact, I was open for more opportunities to serve others. That cup of coffee cost less than a dollar. The time the man spent allowing me to go first in line was less than a minute. Yet, that less-than-a-minute and less-than-a-dollar created a significant ripple effect. I continued doing good for others that entire day. And certainly a number of those people I touched in turn did the same by continuing the spirit of giving. Seek out opportunities to give gifts of less-than-a-minute or less-than-a-dollar.

At Zaclon, employees were asked to create a variety of ways they could make positive contributions to make a difference at the company. Before they went home, they were told that all employees would receive a gift of fun.

At a meeting, a member passed out peanuts in a shell with individual memos that said, "Sometimes I feel like a nut."

Clever, creative, novel approaches break through tired rituals of behavior and training. They encourage people to look beyond boundaries and risk trying novel ideas. When internalized, they encourage openness to having and accepting new approaches to problem solving.

> On the starting blocks before my first Olympic race, I was smiling because I was having fun. That's what it was all about—to have fun.
>
> —Janet Evans, Swimmer
> Three-time Olympic Gold Medalist

☆ *BRIGHT SIDE ENERGIZER* ☆

This is a novel or playful way I can stretch and serve others:

Chapter Nine

"I Think I Can"

They can because they think they can.
—Virgil

We can help our children build positive experiences to bolster confidence at very early ages. These occasions become powerful motivators.

When my daughter was in kindergarten, she brought home a picture she had drawn in school that day. It was a picture of her looking up at a tree and crying. I asked her to tell me about the picture. She lamented that she couldn't climb a tree and that other school friends could. I was heartbroken to hear her disappointment and defeat. I asked her if she ever tried to climb a tree. "No," she responded. Then I asked her how she could possibly know whether she could climb a tree if she had never tried. She looked at me hopefully. I realized my daughter had a self-image that was indeed limiting and that had put her at age five into a state of near helplessness. I knew, however, that she had brought me a challenge I could indeed help her with.

I then remembered a graceful tree in our front yard that was large but not intimidating. So out we proceeded to the tree. I encouraged her to climb the tree. What childlike faith and trust! She decided to tackle the tree and up the tree she went. My experience of running the race in my Red Ball Jets guided what I said to her. I kept encouraging her until she reached the very top!

"You did it!" I congratulated her. She beamed.

Then she asked, "How do I get down?" I stopped. How would she get down? I responded differently, saying that she would come down in the same way she used to get up there. I knew she could do it. I told her that climbing down is a completely different experience, requiring some very serious calculation. Slowly, she proceeded down. Each step of the way, I told her what a great job she was doing. Oh, how I wanted to grab her and help her, but my experience with the Red Ball Jets told me to keep encouraging her. And I did. Maressa did make it up the tree and down! What a magnificent success she felt! Whenever she is uncertain of a new challenge, I remind her about that tree and tell her, "Yes, you can."

The next picture Maressa drew was one of a jubilant little girl, smiling and climbing. Embedded deeply in her mind is yes, you can, just like "The Little Engine That Could."

The memories that we use today affect our current motivation. Because so many of us come from dysfunctional families (my mother married three alcoholics; my father died as a result of his alcoholism), we tend to replay past experiences that reinforce our lack of worth rather than those that emphasize our individual worth and greatness. We have rarely heard, as Maressa did, positive words of encouragement.

To the extent that we believe a past experience is valid, we believe it of ourselves in the future. In Bright Side seminars, "past positives" are expanded in a way similar to Allison Roe's mental picturing process.

Rediscovery of any past positive can trigger individual, team, or organizational excellence. For example, at Zaclon, employees began their meetings in a positive, exuberant, and lively manner with all members retelling a past positive experience and wearing a name tag with their positive nickname. These nicknames are related to a past positive experience. Although it may seem a little corny, it is an excellent way to build spirit, to get people focused on being positive, and to build closer, more intimate relationships.

Zaclon employees are listed in the phone directory according to their nicknames from their past positive experience. It generates a sense of fun. Most significantly, the past positive experiences and nicknames help turn negative thinking into positive energy and motivation, both at work and at home.

Recall this past positive whenever you feel negative, tense, or anxious. Use it to create a sense of energy or spirit before a special event or a meeting.

It is the wonderful child who lives within us who is the healthiest component of who we are. That inner child is filled with adventure, experimentation, curiosity, creativity, hope, joy, and enthusiasm. That wonderful child is the healthiest, clearest, part of us.

Some of us learned as children that we were unworthy. We learned as children that our individual differences were not acceptable. We learned defensive behavior and dysfuntional behavior from our authority figures. It is that defensiveness and dysfunction that has created a barrier to accessing this vibrant kid that lives within. It is through having fun and being playful that we can be reunited with that healthy inner child.

It is heartwarming to see how adults respond when they begin to release their own inner child. It's a sign of acceptance of their own individuality. When I traveled across the United States presenting Bright Side's programs to employees of Progressive Insurance Company, the purpose was to encourage their people to have fun, to play, and to release that wonderful child within. I remember my first presentation, uncertain as to how all these adults would respond to cheers, stickers, and stars.

But afterward, I realized how starved adults are for wellness, play, and fun-filled opportunities in their work environment. Very easily I could see the energy level soar. It is heartwarming to see adults say "I'm awesome, you're awesome, we're awesome!" It's good to see them blow balloons together, putting their negative ideas inside them and letting them all go.

So often we confuse play and fun with the sports that we enjoy. Basketball, tennis, ice skating, or golf are all very enjoyable, but they have little to do with having fun.

And laughing! When we play together, when we laugh together, we build relationships. We connect to each other in a very deep way, without any barriers. That is what creates a real sense of heart and spirit within an organization.

There are playful, relaxing, and energizing methods for encouraging peak performance that are being used by people who have attended Bright Side seminars, like the "Awesome" cheer mentioned earlier. The word can be changed to any other positive adjective ("original," "exceptional," etc.) to describe ourselves in a very effective way. And there is "shake off stress," which is simply moving around playfully, shaking off any stress or tension. It's really motion that changes emotion.

These and all the energizing methods described in this book are good for the mind, the body, the spirit, yet so many people are closed to them. It may be that we are too comfortable with the learning from our childhood and the authority figures in our lives that socialized and conditioned us. We have been shaped by those who threw "ought to" statements at us: "You ought to be this way." However, that socially conditioned part of us can be changed because we can change our learning, even if changing our learning is a very slow, tedious, and difficult process.

This idea was best captured by supervisor Tom Wickwire. Tom related an experience of being taught to read as a young child. The first step was learning to read by using a pointer finger. The second phase was being taught not to use the pointer finger because he was told it interfered with reading. Years later, Tom took a speed-reading course where he was taught again to use a pointer finger, exactly the opposite of what he had been taught years previous. He likened this erroneous learning from childhood to the other negative, limiting habits and beliefs we were taught as children. Any new or contradictory behavior is uncomfortable simply due to its unfamiliarity. He concludes that as the habits of learning the speed reading required repetition to break through wrongly formed habits, so do the new habits of building goodness and trust.

Gregg Searle and I met one year following the Bright Side seminars that he had attended. Formerly an IBM manager, now executive vice president of Interbold, an IBM-Diebold venture, Searle described how he used some of the Bright Side tools and techniques. First, Searle gave stars to his secretary in a novel way. When he was pleased with her work, he would place a star on the documents and then would slip it in the mail to her. On another occasion, Searle was disappointed with a report submitted by one of his colleagues. He conveyed that the report had not been well thought out and that his associate could definitely do much better. The next report was absolutely sensational and earned a Bright Side awesome sticker.

At large IBM meetings, Searle recognized peak performance by distributing baseball tickets with stars. Searle also reminisced about an IBM branch that was ranked as one of the lowest performing nationally. He focused on teaching this branch to believe in themselves and their potential. He emphasized playing loose, not being overly serious, having fun. This new attitude allowed this nonperforming branch to undergo a major turnaround, and become the top-ranked branch in the Midwest.

Then Searle smiled and told me how he used Bright Side's ''awesome'' with his ten-year-old daughter. His daughter was thoroughly frustrated in one particular subject, not doing well. He recalled how my son's soccer team had used ''awesome'' to capture the basketball championships.

Searle decided to give that power word to his daughter. He suggested she recite ''awesome'' whenever she felt tight or anxious. He combined the power ''awesome'' word with a fist-hand movement. Each time his daughter struggled to remember the correct answer, he coached her to break through the fear by saying ''awesome'' and moving her fist. He also instructed her to anchor-in the correct answer by repeating the same ''awesome'' procedure. That is how they studied the night before the test. She thought her father silly, but she did as he recommended. The next morning, the day of the test, Searle placed a Bright Side awesome sticker on her shirt. The outcome: ''Awesome!'' as she said, earning a grade of 100 percent in a subject that used to trouble her!

My friend Jeanne is a tiny, vibrant woman. As a child, she had rheumatic fever. Unable to attend school, taking large doses of prednisone, Jeanne became very heavy. A year later, when she returned to school very overweight, she was ostracized by her classmates. Her weight had become a barrier to acceptance by her peers. The once well-liked and popular Jeanne experienced peer isolation for the remainder of her junior high and high school years even though she soon lost weight and returned to her once normal size. Her classmates, perhaps even Jeanne herself, had an image of when she was heavy that stuck and interfered in her entire public school history.

She saw an opportunity for a change when she went to college. One person saw her high school picture and said she looked like a winner. She never forgot that person's positive regard for her and chose to believe it. It empowered her, filling her with confidence to once again be the lovable, active, and high-performing Jeanne. As she broke through the limiting, negative self-portrait she had painted as a twelve-year-old, she was spurred on to peak performance. What mental images, experiences, words do we internally paint that anchor us in a self-defeating pattern? What images or thoughts do we choose to believe about ourselves?

I love running. One hot summer day, I was doing my usual end-of-the-day run and I passed a man who was gardening. The man said to me, "Persevere!" Now I was grateful to hear such a positive and encouraging remark. I thought to myself about how important perseverance and endurance are. And I thought of the many people who endured no's and rejection because they passionately believed in their dreams. Historical examples are Abraham Lincoln and Thomas Edison. Modern-day heroes may include Jesse Jackson or General Norman Schwarzkopf. And so, on that run, I repeated to myself: "Persevere!" Minutes later, during that very same run, on that very hot day, I passed another gardener who said, "That's too hard to do." I realized I could choose not to believe the negative suggestion made by that second person. Discard, throw away negative suggestions. Choose to believe in good. Choose to believe in goodness. Choose to believe in your own goodness.

Life is like running. Like running on a mountain. And you can choose many paths for your life adventure. And when you choose a path, persevere! And endure! You may be only one foot from the top!

I spoke at the National Conference for Laughter and Play some years ago and I had the opportunity to speak at the same conference with Dr. O. Carl Simonton, the author of *Getting Well Again*. He is a radiologist who is an expert in the area of cancer. Dr. Simonton used the example of juggling in his presentation.

He said that he spent many years thinking he could not juggle. He had defined juggling as when you had a number of objects suspended in the air at the same time. However, he found out that tossing even one object can be considered juggling. And so in this presentation, he passed out marshmallows for people to juggle.

He said the whole secret to juggling was not focusing on the catch, because that's how we become fearful. Rather it's focusing on the toss. That's the way we build a sense of confidence. I want to suggest to you that same kind of thinking pattern—focus on the toss and not on the catch.

Following a Bright Side seminar, a woman told me about her childhood in the mountains of Italy, where she learned to trust her ability to travel narrow ledges on a steep mountainside. As a young child, she did this alone by listening to, trusting, and following the encouraging coaching of her mother. She said that memory from her childhood is a significant component of her self-confidence.

Now, not often do you or I have the opportunity to build self-confidence by climbing steep mountains, although some days we feel that way! Yet, we each have many successes—even many simple successes—like learning how to drive a car; climbing a tree and being able to get right back down; putting together a business deal; fixing a wonderful meal.

Today, I want you to make a list of your successes. Begin with the small successes of life. Keep adding to this success list throughout the entire day. Successes that you remember from any time in your life. And of course, the successes that you create today. At the end of the day, applaud yourself. Be grateful for the successes you have discovered and rediscovered. And tomorrow, get on track, begin the day with success, by reading that success list to yourself.

You can begin your success list by reviewing the words following this chapter that describe an energized, peak performance person. Next to each word select a past experience that anchors-in the success, or picture how you would like to be, perhaps by recalling actions of someone you admire. You also may want to draw a circle with radiating lines. In the middle of the circle, write "I am." Then draw out from it radiating lines, forming a sun. On each line write an empowering, awesome adjective that describes how you are and how you can be.

☆ *BRIGHT SIDE ENERGIZER* ☆

Recall your "Red Ball Jets" past positive.

- To begin each day refreshed and renewed, to feel confident and exuberant.
- To strengthen and empower the internal positive interpretation machine during the day.
- When feeling tired, tense, or negative.
- To become energized.
- To break through and replace any imprisoning past negative experience.
- To picture mentally or meditate on to internally strengthen the experience.
- To picture mentally for rebounding from a "failure" or to get psyched up for a challenge.
- To think you can!

Form more specific and detailed mental pictures of past experiences or desired outcomes as needed for personal or professional success and meaning based on the following list of characteristics. You may wish to add or delete qualities to best facilitate your own growth. . . .

• *Positive Selves*

When negative, use pencil and "let go." Replace and "fill" with positive experiences, using colored markers or crayons. When you lack a concrete personal experience, envision a behavior of a role model. Anchor-in the positive mental picture by drawing a symbol or picture.

I am	*Past Experience/ Future Image/Role Model*	*Desired Outcome*
Resilient Self		
Lovable Self		
Truthful Self		
Creative Self		
Leadership Self		
Achieving Self		
Accepting Self		
Successful Self		
The Bright Side Self		
Joyful Self		
Trusted Self		
Risk-taking Self		
Courageous Self		
Good Student Self		
Learning Self		
Rich Self		
Confident Self		
Hardworking Self		
Persistent Self		
Intuitive Self		
Secure Self		
Caring Self		

I am	*Past Experience/ Future Image/Role Model*	*Desired Outcome*
Responsible Self		
Playful Self		
Humorous Self		
Fit Self		
Worthy Self		
Spiritual Self		
Championship Self		
Joyful Self		
Creative Self		
Serving Self		
Coaching self		

Chapter Ten

Intuition

> The one thing we can trust is our mind, our intuition, our experience.
>
> —Abraham Maslow

Some time ago, my son was in the hospital and was diagnosed as having diabetes. The weekend he was released from the hospital was a joyful one. Sunday morning, we decided to walk several blocks into our village for breakfast. As we returned home, it began to sprinkle. It was a light and gentle spring rain. Both my daughter and son were delighted by the soft raindrops. They played under the light coat I was wearing. I delighted in their laughter. I was grateful that Brant was once again home, doing much better under the control of insulin.

A few moments later, after those thoughts of peace, we were deluged without warning by a fierce rainstorm. Soaked by the downpour, I was miserable. Now I was lamenting our predicament and feeling waves of irritation well up inside of me. My children were in ecstasy, laughing and skipping. Their glee irritated me more as I began to think about the details of changing clothes in order to go to church, wondering if we would be on time, and the nuisance of it all. Then I heard my children laugh louder and begin to sing the song "Singing in the Rain." Perhaps it was the laughter, remembering the catchy Gene Kelly tune, or perhaps it was the rain that cleared my brain, but I realized at that moment that I could not do a thing about the circumstances. But I could do something about my response to it. So I decided to join my children.

The three of us laughed, skipped, danced, and sang . . . in the rain! It was a freeing, joyful moment, feeling totally cleansed of any irritation or negativity. (Incidentally, my neighbor saw us skipping home only to wish he had had his videocamera out.)

That night, I had a dream about storms. In my dream, there was blackness and I recall thinking that this darkness symbolized the storms of life, the challenges that we all face. Then, in the middle of this darkness, there appeared a beautiful, ruffled, multicolored rainbow-colored umbrella. I said to myself in the dream that the rainbow umbrella is like the hope in life . . . the opportunity that comes out of any struggle or crisis. I next wished for an umbrella just like that . . . a colorful symbol for Bright Side.

That week, I made a presentation at a hospital. In setting up for the program, I passed the hospital gift shop. For the first time in my life I heard the quiet inner voice that we hear people talk about. Quite surprised to actually be aware of an inner voice, I was directed to go inside the gift shop to find the rainbow-colored umbrella from my dream. How outrageous, I thought! First, to hear an inner voice and then to even consider going into a gift shop to find an umbrella I dreamed about! Absolutely absurd! Yet, there I stood outside the gift shop, contemplating what to do. After all, I pondered, a bright, educated woman even thinking about looking for something from her dream was pretty crazy!

After some struggle, I mustered up the courage to go into the gift shop to ask for the umbrella from my dream. It was glorious, sunny day—not a rain cloud in sight. In the shop, I was greeted by the storekeeper. Not ordinarily subdued by nature, I shyly asked her if she had any umbrellas. Her eyes lit up and she said that she had only one umbrella left and that she would get it for me. I waited just a few moments, and out she brought the umbrella! An umbrella identical to the one in my dream, a fully ruffled rainbow-colored umbrella.

I got that umbrella only by listening to that quiet inner voice, my intuition. And it was absolutely identical to the one in my dream!

It doesn't make sense, but when we listen to our intuition, it works! Yet, how often do we not trust and listen to our inner voice because it is not logical or proper. Think of the countless times we haven't listened and we wished we had. Think of the countless solutions we have overlooked because we didn't trust our own inner sense.

According to psychologist Carl R. Rogers, "One of the basic things which I was a long time in realizing, and which I am still learning, is that when an activity feels as though it is valuable or worth doing, it is worth doing. Put another way, I have learned that my total organismic sensing of a situation is more trustworthy than my intellect.

"All of my professional life I have been going in directions which others thought were foolish, and about which I have had doubts myself. But I have never regretted moving in directions which 'feel right' even though I have oftentimes felt lonely or foolish.

"I have found that when I have trusted some inner nonintellectual sensing, I have discovered wisdom in the move. In fact, I have found that when I have followed one of these unconventional paths because it felt right or true, then in five or ten years many of my colleagues have joined me, and I no longer need to feel alone in it."

In our society, it is rare for people to share what is really important:

- Our tender inner self
- Our sweet inner self
- Our fragile feelings
- Our creative self

Certainly, the major health problem today is stress. It is heightened by alienation from self and others, and our lack of authenticity and spontaneity. This blocks our ability to be intimate and sensitive with ourselves and those around us.

When we are blocked, our needs are not met, and our positive energy becomes toxic and turns into distress or dysfunctional behavior. We become defensive and swing into behavior of rejecting, judging, criticizing, withdrawing, and hostility. We use a protective shield of logic. A focus of logic keeps us emotionally distant and out of the creative right hemisphere of the brain. Logic causes us to focus on facts and avoid feelings. Yet feelings are absolutely essential to motivation, intimacy, intuition, creativity. William James wrote, "Individuality is found in feeling." Yet, people in our society are uncomfortable with feelings and intuition. The dysfunctional habits we have learned block our sensitivity to feelings and to intuition. We generally feel awkward putting credence in emotions or intuition—yet our most powerful source of intimacy, motivation, customer caring and creativity is emotion and intuition.

The superficial masks we wear distance us from ourselves and others. The critical self constantly repeats those negative statements we have learned that teach us not to feel or rely on our intuition:

- Don't cry.
- Don't whine.
- Don't speak to me that way.

- Don't be selfish.
- Mind your own business.
- Stop acting, feeling, thinking, talking that way.
- Don't pay attention to that.
- Don't be so sensitive.
- Don't be so serious.
- He didn't mean what he said.
- Pretend like you didn't hear, see, feel . . .

Bright Side participants are often touched by the Bright Side rainbow umbrella story, especially when I produce the colorful and ruffly umbrella. I have been pleased to see participants tenderly take the umbrella and do a wonderful rendition of "Singing in the Rain."

I have heard hundreds of stories from people about meeting spouses, avoiding tragedy, and being at the right place at the right time, as a direct result of paying attention to the quiet inner voice, listening to intuition or to our Higher Power. Indeed, as we seek our successes in business, science, or the arts, we often find those achievements were first pictures or ideas that came from our own rich inner treasure.

Creative geniuses like Mozart, Kipling, physicist Neils Bohr, mathematician Henri Poincaré, Goethe, and Brahms spoke of their discoveries as being inspired by intuition, mental images, or a divine source. It is easy to conclude that many of our treasured experiences or valued inventions come from trusting the thoughts, ideas, or images that are produced from within our creative being.

I believe this is something that we can access and utilize daily, not just occasionally. When filled with apprehension, tension, or mistrust, it is often difficult to be aware of such an internal happening. Certainly of help in reaching a deeper level of self or self-awareness is solitude, or quiet, which can usually be achieved through prayer or meditation.

In a world that is filled with the distractions of media, advertisements, and busy work it is often difficult to listen to this internal voice. When the input is diffused, we are not utilizing this rich inner treasure. We not only are not planting healthy thinking seeds, but we are not tending to the fruit that wants to ripen within. The fruit we bear are great ideas, or the special gifts, like the rainbow umbrella, that we can receive in only one way—by listening to and trusting the quiet inner sense.

Yet, when we utilize this inner sense, we receive gifts that we could receive from no other source. Best said by Carl Rogers, "The action of the child inventing a new game with his playmates; Einstein formulating a theory of relativity; the housewife devising a new sauce for the meat; a young author writing his first novel; all of these are, in terms of our definition, creative, and there is no attempt to set them in some order of more or less creative."

Other times, the voice is simply a message to keep us on track. That is how I felt when I saw a garbage truck on the highway with the model name Goliath. I thought to myself that if that Goliath message was for me, then certainly I would have a David in my day. Sure enough, there was a phone call from a David of a Fortune 500 company, just as I entered my office. I began to wonder what David and Goliath could mean for me.

My son was reading *Sounder*, a book that deals with racial prejudice. The boy expressed his fury, feeling like a small David ready to slay the malicious white prison guard, huge in physical power, just like Goliath. It was through a small boy and a slingshot that Goliath was destroyed.

In Bright Side philosophy, Goliath is destructive, negative garbage thinking. David, on the other hand, is the tools of love, emotion, play, and creativity so desperately needed in today's corporate world, as defensive communication halts intimacy and relationships; hinders creativity and intuition; and further estranges the tender inner child.

☆ *BRIGHT SIDE ENERGIZER* ☆

Trust your rich inner essence. Keep record of the great ideas or images that come to you from listening to and trusting your quiet inner voice and intuition:

____

____

____

Chapter Eleven

Coloring and Creativity

> The music of ''Madam Butterfly'' was dictated to me by God. I was merely an instrument in putting it on paper.
>
> —Giacomo Puccini

Boundaries begin even before we learn to color within the lines. I'm reminded of lyrics to ''Flowers Are Red,'' by Harry Chapin, given to me by a friend:

> The little boy went first day in school, he gets crayons and he started to draw.
> He put colors all over the paper, all colors was what he saw.
> And the teacher said, ''What you doing young man?''
> ''I'm painting flowers,'' he said.
> She said, ''It's not the time for art young man, and flowers are green and red.''
> But the little boy said, ''There are all colors in the rainbow, so many colors in the morning sun.
> So many colors in the flower, and I see every one.''
> Well, the teacher said, ''You're sassy. There are ways that things should be and you'll paint flowers the way they are, so repeat after me.''

And she said, ''Flowers are red young man, green leaves are green.
There's no need to see flowers any other way than the way they always have been seen.''
But the little boy said again, ''There are so many colors in the rainbow, so many colors in the morning sun.
So many colors in the flower, and I see every one.''
Well, the teacher put him in a corner. She said, ''It's for your own good.
And you won't come out until you get it right and responding like you should.''
Well, finally he got lonely, frightened thoughts filled his head.
And he went up to that teacher and this is what he said.
And he said, ''Flowers are red, and green leaves are green.
There's no need to see flowers any other way than the way they always have been seen.''
Of course, time flew like it always does. They moved to another town.
And the little boy went to another school. This is what he found.
The teacher there is smiling. She said, ''Painting should be fun.
And there are so many colors in the flower, so let's use every one.''
But that little boy painted flower of rose, green and red.
And when the teacher asked him why, this is what he said.
And he said, ''Flowers are red, and green leaves are green.
There's no need to see flowers any other way than the way they always have been seen.''

These words so poignantly address the loss of our unique, colorful, creative self. How sad that our risk-taking wonder, creativity, and intuition are stifled and snuffed out!

In their book *Build Your Brain Power*, Arthur Winter, M.D., and Ruth Winter write, "Creativity is one of the most marvelous products of the 'fit' brain." They go on to quote Frederick M. Flack, M.D., a psychiatrist, who said: "Creativity is not just a product or an act, but a way of viewing and reacting in new and constructive ways. You have to adapt and readapt to your environment, at home, at work, and in your relationships. You also have to trust your intuition. Intuition is quite different from impulsiveness. It involves perceiving something along preconscious routes frequently bypassing ordinary logic. It is often an artist's or writer's intuition that make masterpieces." As we can see from his emphasis, we have a major need to create.

Flack also maintains, "The person who is creative has the ability to envision things in different ways to have a fresh outlook."

To help Bright Side participants have fresh outlooks, I introduce a kneaded eraser as "gray matter" (a fit brain!). I ask participants individually to come up with as many different uses, functions, titles, and names as they can in a three-minute time period. They are asked to count the number of ideas when finished.

Participants either freeze or relax during this exercise. Those who freeze and become overly serious generate between three and five ideas. Those who relax and become playful come up with ten to twenty.

I then ask participants to form groups of six to eight people. First, they are to collectively count their total number of ideas. This total generally ranges from eighteen to thirty. They are then given another three minutes to generate another twenty-five to thirty brand-new uses or titles. Participants are usually apprehensive, wondering how they can possibly generate even more ideas.

But this attempt is a team effort. The teams are usually successful, sometimes producing a quantity greater than requested.

When there are four or five teams or more, it is not uncommon for the results of the exercise to exceed one hundred to two hundred fresh ideas, a wonderful surprise to most Bright Side participants. At Zaclon, when the company was financially challenged, Joe Turgeon and Jim Krimmel would recall how easy it was for them to create hundreds of "gray-matter" uses. They bridged the learning from that exercise to create solutions for a new and successful financial strategy.

In *Build Your Brain Power,* the Winters offer these exercises to stimulate the brain for creativity:

- Name all the kinds of dogs you can eat.
- Fill in: Her eyes were as green as_______.
- Write, within three minutes, every word you can think of that begins with *y*.
- Make as many different things as you can out of circles and squares.

The following creativity-enhancing techniques from *Build Your Brain Power* are based on the work of Dr. Flack, Dr. Morris Stein, and other experts.

PREPARE YOURSELF. Do as much reading and talking as you can about what you want to create—a solution, a picture, a new approach to a business. Do your homework.

INCUBATE. We all want quick solutions, but when the answers don't come right away, put the thought aside. Let it simmer in your subconscious. At a later point, perhaps a week or month later, there will be a breakthrough.

ILLUMINATE. In cartoons, this is depicted by a light bulb over the head. It is the point when the breakthrough occurs. You let it happen. Something pops into your head and you say, "Ah, that's a good idea."

TEST. Now that you've come up with the creative solution, you have to apply it. If there is a new way to handle your marriage, for example, put it into practice. If you have a new way of creating a sculpture, do it. Dr. Flack says that nobody gets the Nobel Prize for a new idea. One gets it for testing the idea and showing that it works.

DISTANCE YOURSELF. You can do this merely by changing the room in which you are working or your clothes. You can take a "mental excursion" by thinking about a pleasant trip you took or a place you'd like to go. Look at pictures far removed from your ordinary interests or work.

HAVE A VARIETY OF LEISURE PURSUITS. Don't spend your leisure time at one avocation, such as tennis or watching TV. Get a variety of experiences. Meet new people. Read new books. Primarily, leisure should relax you. It is hard to be creative when you are tense. And by avoiding routine—tennis only or TV only—you gain the stimuli of various people and environments and you use a variety of your muscles and talents. Variety is fertilizer for creativity.

FIND SECURITY. It is very difficult to be creative if you are worried about survival. You need to find someone on whom you can depend. Anxiety blocks the free flow of creativity.

DON'T PLAY A ROLE. If you select a role such as the man-in-the-gray-flannel-suit or the superwoman, you get locked in and can't do things another way.

CHOOSE YOUR ASSOCIATES CAREFULLY. If you associate with people who are constantly tearing you down, criticizing you, you won't be able to create.

DON'T BE AFRAID TO BE ALONE. If you are to be creative, you need time to listen to your inner self instead of someone or something else.

TRY TO TURN DOWN YOUR MOTOR. You need some inactive and quiet time to let your thought processes work. That means daydreaming, a form of mental activity frowned upon by parents and teachers—yet it is useful and may open up new channels. You can also reminisce and allow past successes to flow through your mind for reevaluation.

KEEP A PENCIL AND NOTEBOOK HANDY. You can capture fleeting ideas that may later prove to be valuable. You never know what connections may be made between what is novel to you and what you ordinarily have to do.

FIND YOUR BEST TIME. You are influenced by your biological rhythm. There is a time of day or night when you are at your best. You probably know it, but if you want to make sure, it is probably the time when your body temperature is highest.

FIND YOUR BEST PLACE. Try to remember where you got your best ideas. Some people like to think in a warm bathtub and others while walking or while working with their hands.

WRITE OR TAPE YOUR FRUSTRATIONS. When you are feeling frustrated or tied up in knots and the ideas won't come, write or record what is bothering you. It will help "clear the decks" for action.

FARM YOUR BRAIN. Verbalize or write down as many ideas as you can dig out of your brain. Let your mind wander and consider all sorts of solutions. You can help yourself till the fertile soil by making analogies. For example, "I want to paint a better picture, but it is like squeezing the last bit of toothpaste from the tube."

"CREATIVE DAWNING." In this technique (which has been called other names) you put your goal in the center or "sun" and then try to think of as many ideas as you can—no matter how crazy—that could help you achieve your goal. Put those ideas in the rays around your dawning sun.

DEFER JUDGMENT. Really listen to your own thoughts, but don't judge your ideas right away. Don't say, "That's foolish" or "That won't work." By offering negative adjectives, you block the flow of ideas. Keep coming up with solutions no matter how crazy they may sound. Quantity will eventually produce quality.

DON'T BE AFRAID TO MAKE MISTAKES. If you fail, learn what doesn't work. Try a new approach. If you are not failing, you are not being very creative, because new trails are unmarked and full of pitfalls.

DON'T MAKE EXCUSES. Age, infirmity, lack of time (lack of money) are frequent reasons given for not being able to create. They are rarely valid. Picasso, at 91, kept art supplies by his bed in case he awoke during the night and had a good idea. He could then capture it on paper. George Bernard Shaw wrote "The Millionairess" in his eighties. The output of composer Gabriel Faure (1845–1924) increased in quantity and quality during his eighth decade of life even in the face of severe sensory impairment.

I absolutely love my children's Anti-Coloring book by Susan Striker. Such books encourage fresh and original thinking. Some of the exercises are frivolous and fun, others stimulating and challenging: build a fort out of snow . . . construct a factory for the kind of business you would like to own . . . you are very rich, erect a luxury tent for camping in the woods . . . these ants have just started constructing a utopia . . . the old train station was torn down, and you have been asked to design a new one . . . build a tree house where you can go to be alone.

Well, grab your box of crayons: Remember . . . you are awesome. Using all of the colors you have available . . . draw a picture of that precious, wonderful kid who lives within you. That is Bright Side at work!

☆ *BRIGHT SIDE ENERGIZERS* ☆

In Bright Side presentations, the toys are presented to help participants relax, get creative, release the inner child, focus on positives and success, become playful and daydream, break out of routine habit and the fear of making mistakes.

Other Ideas for Creativity

- Playful story building, saying the first thing that comes to mind, is fun and freeing.
- Try ten jumping jacks.
- Give a standing ovation.
- Deep breathe.
- Read a cartoon.
- Mail a cartoon to a friend or associate.
- Tell a funny story about yourself.
- Bring funny ideas to a meeting.
- Walk backwards.
- Blow bubbles (or play with any novel toy).
- Jump rope . . . for fun!
- Swim in a duck pond!
- Practice touching and smiling.
- Find a children's playground . . . try the swing, the slide, or the merry-go-round!
- Draw colorful pictures.
- Bring baby pictures to a meeting.
- Draw a colorful picture about your ideas or vision.
- Draw pictures of your team members during a meeting. (Imagine how they looked and what they were like when they were kids.)
- Draw a stick-figure picture of your ''creative-self'' using your nondominant hand.

- Stand, sit, walk, or move in playful, different ways.
- Play with balloons.
- Read something written for kids. (Even read it to begin a meeting.) Here is one I love.

Eight Balloons

Eight balloons no one was buyin'
All broke loose one afternoon.
Eight balloons with strings a-flyin',
Free to do what they wanted to.
One flew up to touch the sun—POP!
One thought highways might be fun—POP!
One took a nap in a cactus pile—POP!
One stayed to play with a careless child—POP!
One tried to taste some bacon fryin'—POP!
One fell in love with a porcupine—POP!
One looked close in a crocodile's mouth—POP!
One sat around 'til his air ran out—WHOOSH!
Eight balloons no one was buyin'—
They broke loose and away they flew,
Free to float and free to fly
And free to pop where they wanted to.

—Shel Silverstein
From *A Light in the Attic*

Chapter Twelve

"Bright Side at Work"

An Interview with Nancy Vetrone
Founder and President
Original Copy Centers, Inc.

I don't have good business skills. I have good people skills.
Nancy Vetrone

Nancy Vetrone is founder and president of Original Copy Centers, Inc. It was the first print-for-pay copy center in Ohio and has been recognized as the largest copy center in North America by *Quick Printing* magazine. Actually, it has customers around the world.

Original specializes in the reproduction of books and manuals on an overnight or short turnaround basis. It can also reproduce one million letter-size impressions overnight. Vetrone's business has been on the Inc. 500 list of fastest-growing private companies in America for four years in a row—from 1986 to 1989. She has been recognized by Ernst & Young as "Entrepreneur of the Year."

Vetrone's company has taken the mundane commodity service business of making photocopies and turned it into a high-tech, profitable business of black-on-white document management services for the corporate market. Its goal is to help manage the proliferation and reproduction of documents in urban office environments. Simply put: "to help people communicate."

The company is also a Bright Side client. I recently interviewed Vetrone about her company, herself, and the value of Bright Side ideals in business.

DS: As we began talking, you got a phone call. What did the caller want?

NV: They were dealing with numerous subcontractors, and we were the only ones that truly had customer service. They said we got a job out for them over the weekend. It was a good-size job, and the customer service rep was right there and took care of everything for him. He said we were a "very service-oriented company."

DS:. Did the caller explain why he thought you were the only company that really was customer service–oriented?

NV: He said all the other vendors seemed to give the reasons why they couldn't get something done. We were the only ones who found a way to do it.

DS:. How have you ingrained the yes attitude in the minds of your employees?

NV: It sounds simple, but it is in selling them on being part of the team. We do not currently have any commission salespeople, because we feel the selling end, or the customer service end, is just a piece of the whole pie.

No piece here is more important than the other. I think when you have commission sales, you start finding that salespeople don't necessarily sell for the good of all concerned, which is our company philosophy.

DS:. So you really have seen a difference since Bright Side in terms of how your salespeople interact with your customers?

NV: Yes, definitely. I think they are looking out more for the good of the customer. They aren't going to just push through a sale. It sounds like the reverse of what a company should look for, but because they're not pushing to make their commission dollars, they're not going to promise something that really can't be done. They instead truly look at things and ask what they can do to help this person out, so we can keep the customer.

They can't sell anything without the cooperation of everyone in Production, Marketing, and on and on and on. Before, there always was an attitude that the sales area was the most important and the most prestigious. But if you don't have everyone oriented to the same goal, they can sell until they're blue in the face, and it'll get harder and tougher for sales eventually. I think in a lot of companies, sales is the part that doesn't buy into the team concept.

DS:. Did you have resistance to changing from a commission structure to a salary structure?

NV: We're working on an incentive plan. We're taking away from dollar volume and putting it into unit volume, so the whole company can get into the fun of achieving goals. It's based on a common goal of how many units can we put out in a month; that means they have to sell it, the others have to produce it, the billing department has to bill it.

DS:. A lot of people talk about caring about people in general. What are you doing internally to put that message into action?

NV: Well, it has to come from the person on the top. I have never had a belief that anyone is more important than anyone else. Just like myself. I have a job here and my job is to be the "keeper of the culture."

DS:. That's an interesting expression, "Keeper of the Culture!"

NV: I have to make sure my management focuses on the positive and not on the negative. In every other company I've ever worked in, the people who get all the attention are the negative people. They're the ones who create all the problems. My job is to minimize everything that has to do with those negative people. I think they should just be ignored. If I have thirty people over here who are breaking their necks and trying to get things done, why am I so concerned about the one over there who won't pay attention to the rules, or is tardy all the time? I should spend my whole day on the people who are good.

Companies are so unfair to the good people! They tend to be forgotten. Your code of conduct, procedure manual, or anything else is only written for the negative, not the positive one. You do have to have it to protect the company because those negative people come in to take advantage of it.

But then, you make sure that everything else you do, including benefits, is all oriented to the good people. That's why we put in an attendance bonus program. When I put in an attendance bonus, I knew who was going to get the money. It was going to be the good people, who showed up every day. The negative ones, who are giving us a problem, don't get the bonus.

DS:. What is the bonus based on? How does it work?

NV: They have to give us perfect attendance for one quarter, or only sixty working days. We break it down in quarters so that they have an opportunity to make it more than once. If you do end up with the flu and lose it for a quarter, you have three other quarters in the year that you can take advantage of. You can opt either to get $100 or to take a day off with pay. It's your choice. A lot of our managers, from a money standpoint, should be taking the day off with pay but they opt to take the $100 bill because they don't want to miss a day. It gives me an opportunity to reward them for perfect attendance.

DS:. What are some other ways you reward positive behavior and positive attitudes?

NV: Well, I guess it's back to the attention paid to them, and my constant reminder whenever I see one of our managers overdoing it on the negative group. For example, if there's a gossiping problem, they may be spending so much time trying to get to the root of it that they don't go over and pat somebody on the back. Or, a common practice is when you know somebody's good, the easy way out is to give them the more difficult jobs all the time.

DS:. The more challenging jobs?

NV: Yes.

DS:. That can be a reward for some personality types.

NV: Oh, yes it is. But you have to let them know that you are doing that because they are good. Then they feel really great about it. You can't let them ever get the feeling that you're too busy for them and they just get everything thrown at them.

DS:. There is a lot of negativity out in our culture, a lot of defensive behavior. How does an organization begin to move in a more positive direction?

NV: That's a hard one. Life philosophies came somewhat natural to me because of my personality. I'm not greedy. There is a level that I need in order to make my own life nice, but I don't believe in excess. I don't need a lot of stuff. I have a job here like they have a job here. They buy into working for me by realizing that I do share it all, and that I put it back into the company to create more jobs and a nice solid company that is not on the verge of going bankrupt or laying people off. There is no skimming off the top.

I went nine years without a paycheck. That's what happens a lot of times in the struggle of making a business work. By the time you finally do experience making any money, you get out of proportion with it. I think I was fortunate enough that I caught myself. I needed a nice car and I got a nice car, but I only needed one. I have a gold watch, but I don't need two of those either. Everyone here knows how I am. So they can buy into it easier. They don't begrudge me. In other places employees always look at their employer, asking why does he make all of that money, he doesn't do anything? [saying] I'm the one who's doing all the work, I'm the one who's sitting here working all the overtime, and they're just going out and living lavish lives.

They also know I enjoy coming to work. I think that's a real strange phenomenon to a lot of them, that I go around and I preach how exciting it is. I think we are very privileged that we have great jobs. I would never want to be home doing nothing. What would you do with your life if you didn't have a job?

DS:. Do you think you present a message that says that a person's own reason for being can be woven into his or her work?

NV: Oh, I'm sure. I think you're here to be the best possible person you can be, and that includes making a living.

DS:. How do you give your people the opportunity to be the best possible people they can be?

NV: No one stands over them with a whip setting all kinds of unrealistic performance standards. I think everyonc wants to achieve. You just give people the opportunity and you set it in front of them, and you trust them to do it. They'll give you a much better job than if you badgered them into it.

DS:. So what you're saying is, you believe right from the very beginning that every person who comes here really wants to do well, and really wants to be an achiever.

NV: Yes.

DS:. So that kind of sets the tone for this positive environment.

NV: I would agree. If you get a couple of negative people, it seems so easy for them to pull everyone down with them. It can start as simple as, oh I'm so tired today, I don't feel like coming to work. Oh, I wish I didn't have to work, I can't wait until I go home. Then all of a sudden somebody else is complaining.

I tell people I'm not going to put up with it. I worked too darn hard to get this business off the ground. I'm not saying people don't have a down day here and there, but if you have too many of them you don't deserve the job. I'll try to work with you.

Last night, for example, I helped a young man who is usually a very positive guy but all of a sudden we starting noticing negative behavior. I called him up and said, it seems like something's bothering you. Is there anything you want to talk about? It turns out he had some problems. He was short of money and trying to accomplish all kinds of things around the holidays, and didn't have a car and didn't want to tell anybody. To him this was a huge, mammoth problem. Well, we ended giving him an advance on his pay, and he's back to the positive way he was.

I don't want to become a bank for all of my employees, but what is the big deal? This kid has done a heck of nice job for us for a long time. He had a little problem, so we settled it. We've done this same thing before.

DS:. A lot of times, people would even be embarrassed or they would be in denial or they wouldn't want to mix personal and business. How do you pick up on these signs and habits, and how do you have the trust that's so necessary for people to bring these personal problems into their work environment?

NV: We focus on people. Our managers have to be close with their people. They don't have to socialize outside of the building, but they have to have a comfortable relationship with that person. And that person also has to be comfortable with me.

DS:. It really amazes me that you have interceded in that way. That's how trust and caring builds, because there's an example of it. That man you helped will go back and say very wonderful things about you and the whole team.

NV: Right, although he also knows I would never tell people in the company what I did for him. I tell him nobody knows about this except you and me. That's the way it should be. However, people say nice things about you anyway. A lot of people give away money because they want their name on a list. That to me is really very unimportant.

DS:. Let's go back to the point in your life where you picked up these values.

NV: Probably it was based in my childhood. But what changed my life was I was married and had four children; it was a very, very stormy marriage. When I finally got enough nerve to end the marriage, it ended very explosively. He destroyed all the furniture and ripped up all of our clothes and burned them in a big bonfire in the backyard. He did that when I had left one morning to go to my brother's wedding. I discovered it that night when I came home with my four children. I went from having a place to live, clothes, and a pretty decent life-style, to having absolutely nothing by the end of that day. Out of seven or eight rooms, a clothes hamper was the only thing that he had not destroyed. He had taken an ax to the refrigerator and the stove, and he told the insurance company that he had done it, so the insurance company covered nothing.

I remember sitting there and saying, "Well, now what are you going to do?"

Unknown to me, my neighbors had heard him and seen him destroying things for over ten hours and had not wanted to get involved. He had been throwing all the winter clothes and stuff out of the attic window onto the fire. The fire department had come, and warned him not to have bonfires. I can remember sitting there on the clothes hamper, and my children were in shock. And my kids were young—my youngest daughter was only one. That night I ended up staying with my mother. But she lived in a one-bedroom apartment.

I quickly found out who were the phony people in my life. I discovered a lot of people who were only good-weather friends, social friends, but they could care less if somebody was having a problem.

At the time I thought that was the biggest disaster that happened in my life, but looking back three or four years later, I see tremendous strength came out of that. No one would rent to me because I was divorced, and of course I had no furniture, or money for a deposit. I was working, but my job didn't provide enough money to get myself on my feet, let alone buy bare essentials. I went to welfare and was totally turned off. They said I could have, say, $60 for clothes for my children, and I thought you've got to be kidding. I'll do it myself. We lived with the picnic cooler as our refrigerator for almost a year. I would stop on the way home with ice and milk, and that's how we lived.

We knew what our goal was. Our goal was to get our life better. We took one thing at a time. I went out and got three jobs, and my oldest son did the best he could to take care of the smaller kids.

Little by little we bought a chair, then we bought a table. One paycheck went to replace some of our clothes. And one went for what we call our fun money, which was buying something. Then the other one went for rent and food and things.

This taught me a lot about people and a lot about the phoniness in life, where a lot of people think that the whole key is having money, and really, money has so little to do with it. I know so many miserable people with money. The majority of the people who I worked for were miserable people.

I don't live a fancy life. I live, to me, a great life although some people who come over to where I live will say, this is where you live? How much does your company do in sales? They are totally amazed that I have a two-bedroom apartment. But it's enough. I don't need anything bigger. I think I would be very uncomfortable in some big house with all kinds of bedrooms that nobody slept in. It would seem kind of stupid.

DS:. When you used the cooler for one year as your refrigerator, did you view that in a positive way? What were your self-attitudes about that?

NV: To me it was just a solution to the problem. Granted it wasn't perfect, but we had cold milk, and we had ice. It took us a long time to pull ourselves back, but it was amazing to me that my children never had any concept that having the lights or gas shut off was abnormal. They would call me at work and say, the lights are out again. And I said, okay, I'll take care of it. It was not a big deal. And I never overplayed it. They judge you by how you overcome your problems.

DS:. Who came through for you during this time?

NV: I was the one with the most within my family, but they did what they could to help out. That's where I got the mattress from to start out with. One of them gave me the picnic cooler. They did what they could do.

It doesn't resolve suddenly one day, where all of sudden you sit there and say, I guess I have everything I need now. It was just a natural progression. Things did get easier as we got more and as we made more money, and as my positions changed within companies and things like that. That was about a nine- or ten-year span. By the time I decided to open up a company, I had a good credit rating, a very good job, and I was earning decent money.

In a way I went and did the same thing to myself, which was, I laid everything back on the line again and said, okay I'm going to take a chance to go into something bigger, and if I pull this off I will do it differently from others.

DS:. And the skills you learned during this adventure with your kids are the ones you're applying now?

NV: Right. In reality I don't have good business skills. I have good people skills. I suppose you would say I am a terrible businesswoman, because I always look for what is fair, and that's how I do things, for the good of all concerned. Whereas, a good businessman in our society is somebody like Michael Milken, junk bond trader. He's considered a good businessman. He was a star for a long time, and had millions and millions of dollars. The other people known for being good business people are those people who will cut a deal and step on whoever, and they'll nail anyone to the wall. That is how we assess someone being a good business person.

DS:. What is your definition of a good business person?

NV: I am a fair person. I have never done anything unethical. However, I will never let anyone walk on me. There is a fine line.

DS:. You have a good sense of self-esteem.

NV: Right. I'm strong. I don't want to give the impression that I am very weak, but to me a lot of deals seem really stupid. I'm here for the creation of better community. First, I needed to raise my own self-esteem and get myself out of the hole. Then the goal became pulling my children up, then the goal became my first employees and making sure they were in this loop. And then it became more employees and then it became the community which has problems. You just keep furthering this.

DS:. What you're saying is you're helping to raise the standards for a lot of people.

NV: Right. I think anyone who has a job at Original Copy Centers is a privileged person.

DS:. I think so too. I want to go back to this idea of what makes a good business person. What you're describing is greed versus caring. Greed versus loving and giving.

NV: Right. It's almost the negative-positive, that people think that this is really stupid. I have had some males say to me, you will never be successful in business with your attitude. They view it as a weakness that I am so concerned about the people who work for me. To me, it is my positive. I think that's why we're here. We got here because we do a heck of a good job, and we want to do a good job. I bet 95 percent of my people buy into the same philosophy. They are as concerned about our customers as I am about them.

DS:. Did they buy into it after coming here?

NV: Yes, after.

DS:. So in other words, you didn't hire people who have a certain profile?

NV: Oh, God, no!

DS:. You see people change in this environment?

NV: Absolutely. As a matter of fact, we just hired four people who were on welfare. We just made a commitment. Let's take them off of one of the programs and see what we can do with them within our culture here. Two of them we just couldn't convert over. It was just too ingrained in them. They were raised in that for so long they don't have a belief that anything works. But we had two successes who have been promoted over the years, and they've been with us for quite a long time.

We have had all kinds of people working here. No, there isn't a set profile that I look for. Most of the people in our management have gotten where they are through hard work, not through book knowledge. We learn what we need to know when we need to know it.

I don't have a college education nor do I have a great desire to go after one. If I need to know it, I'll find a person who can help me, or I'll find a book on it. I don't claim to know everything about business. But I have enough great people with me that one of us comes up with the idea. I have a great accountant who buys into my philosophy, so therefore I need that great accountant, and I need to have respect for her and her judgment. If I know she is looking at things with my eyes or through my eyes, I don't have any problem. I don't need to go and educate myself to become a great accountant.

DS:. I agree. Now, what is your idea of power?

NV: Power to me would be like class. Class to me has nothing to do with how much money you make and what kind of clothes you're wearing. You're powerful within yourself.

In reality I have power. There are over 150 people here, and I think I have more power than a lot of people who think that they have power. But the fact is I don't need to do anything with it. You know what I'm saying.

DS:. Yes. What about the perception that because you are fair and because you are generous, caring, and positive, that you are weak?

NV: I think that is a perception that is in our society. I think I would reverse it and say that the people who try to come across as powerful are normally the weak ones. They normally come across very strong, almost obstinate. They think they get their power through fear. To me, there are all those old sayings like you catch more flies with sugar than with vinegar, and I definitely believe that. People who take the negative side and say that others take advantage of you never look at the true percentage. They think that if you have 95 percent positive and 5 percent who are going to take advantage, then you're really stupid. It seems to me that if you're smart you're going to go and hang in with the 95 percent, not with the 5 percent.

DS:. When I came here this afternoon I was greeted very nicely, and I would hope that it's because of the things that we have shared in the past, and the way that I have gotten to know everybody. But I also believe your people are friendly to everyone who comes through. Many other times I've been in facilities, and the only one who would offer to give me a tour would be the leader of the company. But when other people come forward and say, oh look at what we're doing, and I want to spend time with you and get to know you, I see those as real powerful benefits to what you're talking about. How many times were you an Inc. 500 winner?

NV: Four times, four consecutive years. But it's actually based upon growth over a five-year period. You have to have very heavy fast growth and be able to sustain fast growth for a five-year period in order to make it for the first year. But then your base always gets higher. It becomes more and more difficult because the multiplier is going to get higher. So it's quite an achievement to be listed for four consecutive years, especially in a service-oriented business like ours. We don't make a set product where everything is custom made, so it's a pretty tough thing to pull off. I heard at one time there were only twelve who had done it.

DS:. What would be the first thing that you would do if you were going into a negative environment of another company?

NV: I'd want to meet whoever is in charge of personnel. Instead of being president, I would probably go in first as the personnel director. Yes, and get to know the people. Start weeding through to see who I thought was salvageable to buy into a culture like mine.

DS:. What if, just if, you didn't have the opportunity to initiate a sift through people?

NV: It would take a long time. If I went into a smaller company and became president, the first thing I would do is to make sure that I had personal meetings with each one of the people. Separately, so that I got to know them. I would be more concerned about getting to know them than getting to know the product. Because the people already have been making the product, if you're about an existing business. I would come about it totally from a personnel angle.

DS:. Building relationships?

NV: Yes, and then instilling them with some of my ideals and values. This is the type of person that I am. I am not asking you to buy it or believe me right now, but you're going to have to open your mind to it, because you're going to see these types of changes happen. And the one thing I tell everyone who is hired here is I'll provide the environment and everything else. You have got to provide the work. Don't ever think for a second that I don't expect you to hold up your end. Don't think that you are going to come in here and have a piece of cake. My standards are very, very high as far as work. So you're going to have to work if you come here. But if you're putting out the work everything else falls into place.

DS:. What would be the next thing that you would do?

NV: Well, it would depend on what kind of business it was. How did I get in this position? Did I buy this company or something?

DS:. Well, really what I'm leading up to is looking at companies who say they want to change, and who say they want to build trust and teamwork. But they wipe out relationships, feelings, and caring, all of the things that you are talking about.

NV: Well, if it is a huge company, they have to break it down into smaller units because I myself know that it's probably around 100 to 150 people per unit. You would have to have a person who buys into your philosophy in charge of each group of say 100 people or 150 people.

DS:. That's a very good idea. Then how would you stop the negative consensus that you described earlier in our interview?

NV: Sit right out in the middle of it. They need to get involved or else it's going to be 95 percent negative instead of 95 percent positive. Be right out on that production floor or right in the middle of the accounting department, or whatever it is that they are in charge of. Don't sit in an office. Be out there, getting to know people, be involved in their everyday working and living.

DS:. Are those qualities you think that come more naturally to a woman?

NV: Yes. I think women are more caring. However, we are not more team oriented. That's the down side of the female personality. We are more caring about those whom we wish to care about, but we are not team oriented normally because we're not nice to our own sex.

DS:. Have you seen that a lot?

NV: Yes.

DS:. Can you give an example?

NV: When I started the business and I was in charge of the sales, I found it was easier to get a job from a male rather than a female, which was totally the reverse of how I thought. I thought I had a 99 percent chance of getting the job from a woman because she would lean a little bit toward me, but I found instead that if you were close to bankruptcy, well, they might throw you some scraps.

Once you started making it, they were jealous, and they did not want to help you make anything of yourself. As the company started making it, our name got around, but I found more and more women got in the way of my getting work out of companies. For some reason, they didn't look at a male as being a competitor, so they would give jobs to a male-owned business rather than a female-owned business. It's really a very strange thing. Women judge women too much by the clothes that they wear and how much money they have and where they live. Petty things.

DS:. How do men judge women?

NV: Normally in my business relationships, they just want the job done. But if you can prove you can do the job, I don't see a big problem. It's hard to get them to give you the first opportunity, but then it's up to you. Show them that you can do the job and they don't change in midstream. They'll hang in there with you.

We hired a young lady to look into a 401K plan for the company. She has her MBA, and I respect her for her education and her knowledge base. I thought this was a good way for her to get to know our people and really get her feet wet. I told her I wanted her to thoroughly research everything, and that I wanted everyone in the company to buy into this thing with gusto.

Later she called and said a man had come in and asked to talk to the decision-maker, so she got me. I said, "I think you're missing something here. You go back in that room and you tell him you are the decision-maker.'' She said he really wanted to talk to the president and I said, ''You are the decision-maker. I put you in charge of this. If he has a problem in dealing with you as the decision-maker, he apparently is not the person we need.'' After the meeting, she came back and said, ''I realize what you just did. You made me accountable for putting in the very best program because I'm the one who has to make that decision and not you.'' And I said, ''Absolutely right. That's what you were hired for. You are not going to use me as your scapegoat.'' And I'll tell you, we have one beautiful plan in here, 95 percent of our people participating, which is unheard of. The company that we went with wants to use us as a role model.

DS: All right. Someone comes to you with a good idea. What do you do with it?

NV: If I think it's a good idea I place the responsibility back on him.

A young lady came over recently. She said she had been a beauty consultant at Estée Lauder. She said she noticed that some of the women here needed some help with their makeup and their hair styling, and she wondered if she could hold a class. I think she thought that I would get the marketing people and set everything up. I said, since you know how to do this, these are the departments that you will have to utilize. If you can pull it off, here's the budget I'll give you. You can put me down as one of the attendees, and just let me know how you're doing.

In two months, out of seventy women we have here, about forty-five or fifty showed up after work for a beauty seminar. She expanded upon it. She contacted different distributors and got little gifts to give away, and she made personal gifts for door prizes. Then she wrote a book. She had our design department put it together, and production put it into a really nice format for her. Marketing put a notice in the newsletter on the boards, but all at her direction. She also had to do her job during this time. It was really a nice event. But so frequently, someone will come up with an idea, and they want to give me the idea and put me in charge of it. That's not what I'm looking for.

DS: Has this woman done anything more since?

NV: She did some personal consultations. Now she has people coming up and asking what kind of eye shadow they should wear. She did take four or five volunteers and show what could be done to enhance them. It was very, very interesting and a lot of fun. She played some games.

We ended probably getting ten times more from the seminar than if I had put it together. When she marketed it, I pointed out that she never put her name on it. She had written it like it was an Original Copy Center event. I said, "This isn't an Original Copy Center event. This is your event. So put your name on it and take our name off of it."

She came in with music, all kinds of things. She was really well prepared and everybody loved it. She heightened my impression of her.

DS: I am curious: what happened to her productivity when she was empowered to do this?

NV: I know nothing slacked off in her department, and I think she is a more positive employee now. She is more accepted and more respected. It's given her more pride.

DS: Have other people been motivated to copy her initiative?

NV: We had another girl who put together a road rally. Again, I told her basically the same thing: she could advertise it in the newsletter and on the bulletin boards. We'll give away T-shirts. But you have to realize I'm not going to be responsible when people are driving in cars. I don't want it to be an Original Copy Center event. This is your event. So you put it together, and if you need some help with the fliers and the printing, we'll help.

DS: And you pay for these things too?

NV: Now I didn't pay for anything with the road rally other than running the fliers and promotion within. With the beauty consulting, I gave her a very nominal budget just to buy some items. I figured she was going to buy makeup, but she got most of it donated, so she ended up making makeup bags for everybody.

DS: And that must have really helped feelings of goodness here. Tell me about the family and friends day.

NV: We nicknamed that Hot Dog Day. We have a Halloween party, which is just fun, on a Sunday night. We have dynamite costumes. It's treated like fun, not a pressure thing. It has more to do with creativity.

DS: How do you equate having fun and creativity?

NV: Well, going to a costume shop and renting a costume to me would not be very creative. One of the real costumes was a group of five of our people who got together and came as black and white copies—11 X 17 copy. It was really neat because they thought about our product. They thought about Original. It wasn't a lot of work and whoever came up with the idea got the others to buy into it.

DS: Do you think that fun influences creativity? How do you build that bridge?

NV: Yes. There is a bridge, maybe creativity isn't the right word for it. Maybe it's just openmindedness. Someone else came as a toothbrush using one of our paper boxes. They made bristles coming out of the top. Then they dressed in a sheet of yellow felt that went up over the box. They used styrofoam to make the bristles of the brush. It was a great outfit.

DS: So you have Friends and Family Hot Dog Day and the Halloween Party?

NV: And Christmas. Normally Christmas is a black tie event. We also place poinsettias all over, and everybody takes them home. The family picnic in the summer is a lot more casual. We also have a day at Cedar Point, where we all take the bus out together.

DS: Oh, you also have anniversary celebrations, and potlucks—right here?

NV: The potlucks are great. For the last one, we invited everyone to bring their favorite dish. We set up tables on the second floor, but we had so many people bring in so much food we had to move into the basement because we didn't have enough room! From that idea, one of the women is doing an Original cookbook of recipes from our own people.

DS: And that's the openness that you were talking about. And if it happens in ways that utilize people's ideas, whether they are about doing a job differently or having more fun and building relationships, it still impacts the bottom line.

NV: Sure. Now some ideas are easier to implement than others. For example, a way to do something differently. When you are under deadline, those are things that are hard to get to. It could be a good idea, but because we are across five shifts, an idea that changes our production has to really be looked at, and we have to get other people to buy into it on other shifts. Those types of things are harder to pull off.

DS: What do you do when that idea comes up and you know it's going to take a little time to assess it?

NV: I would document the idea so that I don't forget to follow up. Then I would invite the head of our production area or whatever area this is from, to come and listen to it.

DS: So ideas are respected?

NV: Right. They are not all initiated, but they are all respected and looked at.

DS: They're not prematurely judged?

NV: No.

DS: What you're really saying is you take care of the heart and spirit of people so that you have a high-quality company, high-quality service, etc.

NV: Right.

DS: As we look at what you're doing versus how other companies do it, I call that garbage stuff out there ''Goliath.'' And I look at what you're doing as David.

NV: True. Although you better make it Nancy, not David.

DS: It strikes me that here's this huge giant that's being overpowered by the kinds of things that you are describing.

NV: Oh, definitely. But Goliath has been in existence a lot longer, so it's bigger. It's everywhere. But does that mean that we shouldn't try it our way?

Chapter Thirteen

Trisking

Man cannot discover new oceans unless he has the courage to lose sight of the shore.

—André Gide
Nobel Prize winner

I had an interesting conversation with a manager of a well-known Fortune 500 company. This corporation had brought me in to build team and relationships, to help shed barriers and fear, to increase trust, and to teach them how to have fun.

The team made strides in reaching their objectives. However, a constant obstacle they faced was lack of trust. This was also evidenced by their people, some of whom did not want to fill out a confidential questionnaire I had introduced. Some of the team managers concluded that the refusal stemmed not from distress or lack of trust, but from many other causes, like lack of insistence from the managers to their subordinates that they finish it. It clearly showed denial, justification, and lack of trust.

When I suggested to this particular manager that this unwillingness reflected dysfunctional behavior and lack of trust within the management team, he quickly agreed. He gave a twenty-five-year history as to why people were not taking risks, and why there was such an abundance of fear and so little trust. This manager related an experience he had had years before. He took a risk, not successful, he said, and his opportunity for advancement was killed. With that one experience, his dreams were killed. He stopped trying. He was blocked. He learned to get ahead, he said, by not risking, even though the current leadership team of this organization is calling people to try new ideas. This manager has chosen to be imprisoned by past experience, limited by something that happened years ago.

I was struck by the way events and people over twenty years before influenced the thinking and behavior of these executives and their staff much in the same way that negative childhood experiences limit us. These past events were reality to an entire organization—to a huge working force of people—and they dictated current behavior that was defensive and thus destructive to any possible organizational gain or momentum. It clearly demonstrated the need for developing people and encouraging individual thinking.

If past negatives from years ago form the thinking, behavior, and environment of one major Fortune 500 company, think how that same toxic thinking is probably permeating many other large and small organizations.

Ted Garver, a well-respected Cleveland venture capitalist and attorney, reminded me of the "trisking" concept I introduced at a CEO meeting. Trisk is a word I learned from wellness expert, John Travis, M.D. It weds two words that are highly touted in today's world: *trust* and *risk*. Trust plus risk is *trisk*.

Trust begins within. Trust is increased by risk-taking, not necessarily physically but rather mentally, emotionally, and spiritually.

Often, the initial step to internal trust building is doing or saying things we have never done or said before, particularly in the face of fear. In Bright Side seminars, participants are encouraged to get into peak performance states by trisking. Energy and confidence are increased when we "let go" of the defensive masks of self-protection. When we protect ourselves, we misuse our energy.

Garver maintains that the primary function of an attorney is to protect people who cannot trust one another. He compares this behavior to that of cavemen, who were continually faced with the fear of death by predatory animals. Today, man does not face death, but the same fierceness of lack of trust and intense fear permeates our thinking. Garver maintains that since we usually do not face a risk factor of dying, we need and can afford to give people all the opportunities necessary to risk and fail because one of the risks will eventually translate into success. That same sentiment is echoed by Jim Krimmel, president of Zaclon, formerly a Du Pont division:

> I think we also tend not to give good positive reinforcement. I also like the card that you handed out to us with that very powerful quote. It says, "Treat a man as he is, and he will remain as he is, treat a man as he can or should be, and he will become as he can or should be." I use it when I look at people now. I don't use it by saying it, although I have said it several times at meetings, when I am trying to get some of our managers to take a risk and give people a little more responsibility when they are not really confident that they are able to handle it. If you treat a man like he can do it, he may fall at first, but then we also say part of our culture, Zaclon culture, is we expect people to take risks. When you take risks you are going to fall occasionally, but if you give them that responsibility and show them you believe they can do it, in time they will. I think that is a very powerful tool.

Garver believes businessmen don't focus on trust because it violates their macho image. Indeed, for many there is a motto:

"Stick it to the other guy anytime you can." People also hide behind a mask of "it is for corporate good" to justify untrustworthy ways.

When there is trust, tasks can be accomplished in one third of the time. Garver suggests that the first step to building trust is to simply focus on building it. In other words, begin to trisk. This can only happen in a place that encourages open and free communication and relationships, where people feel safe in risking their thoughts, creative ideas, and emotions. For many, this is a foreign experience. Yet, I believe this is the path for not only increased trust, self-esteem, and personal empowerment, but also for a successful future at work and in personal relationships. This is how it works at Zaclon, according to Jim Krimmel.

> We've got one individual who was asked to take a look at our solid waste costs, Andy Lewandowski. He has gone far beyond the original scope. He has redefined his assignment. He is contacting vendors nationwide, trying to find out what people are doing, visiting other companies to see what they are doing with their solid waste, in particular lining up demonstrations of equipment. These are the kinds of things that you would expect a project engineer to be assigned to. Well, this is not a project engineer. This is a very involved shipping operator, essentially. That's what he is. I absolutely applaud it. He is doing better than most project engineers doing something like this. We have implemented a couple of his suggestions and will continue to. I see him growing into almost a full-time position of solid waste management in essence. (I hate to use the word management because you try to blur the line between management and hourly people, and to use management in titles is bad, I think.)
>
> Andy Lewandowski has always been a go-for-it kind of a guy anyhow. That's why he was assigned originally to do

> this. It really didn't go anywhere, in my opinion, until we got into this last series of Bright Side. Then he really did reach and stretch and take some risks, and I think we are better for it, he is better for it and I see him growing.

In Bright Side seminars, I help participants focus on being triskers in simple, nonthreatening ways: sharing something they enjoy or like about themselves or each other; sharing something that most people don't know about them; giving positive feedback to one another; placing gold stars in creative, fun, playful (and positive) places on each other; doing things they have never done before, like repeating a Bright Side cheer; accepting diverse opinion; expressing honest emotion. I also encourage participants to focus on trust by recalling experiences when they felt trust for each other, and why. As trust increases, I encourage them also to share the occasions when they felt mistrust. Amie May, executive assistant and office manager of Forest City, developers and operators of shopping malls across America, began building trust in a series of Bright Side seminars. This is how she focused on trust when she returned to work:

> The prior boss didn't trust us. We didn't really fear him but he didn't trust us or our ability to get things done. He spent too much time on small matters instead of the whole picture, which I don't think he ever understood.
>
> For example, there was this gentleman who had come from New York who wanted to take some money out of petty cash. I told him he couldn't do that unless he signed for the money. My boss came out, and in the middle of this huge office, jumped up and down and told me to give him the money, that he would pay it back. Well, I did, and the man never paid it back. The boss had a manager come and check my petty cash to make sure I hadn't taken any money out of it. I was insulted. I would never do that.

> He would also go through your desk, and if he didn't like the way you had things in your desk, you would come in the next morning and everything would be all over the desk. He went into one girl's desk and he didn't like the way she had the carbon paper in there, so he just picked it up and threw it all over the floor. Then he told her to pick it up. Working with him was not a happy experience.
>
> Now I'm much more trusting. I'll take chances. I'll take that risk because of the Bright Side seminars. I remember coming back from the seminars and thinking that old teachings taught us not to trust other people in the work force, to keep everything to yourself. Because of Bright Side I am now more trusting and eager to share what I know with my secretary or my staff. I'm not afraid to do that now. I want them to know so they can be better people and do more in their jobs. Secretaries in particular will ask questions. I used to not share much information, but now I do. I tell them how I got the information and explain the way I went about getting the answers, so the next time they can also do it. Of course, I lost power and control, but that's okay because I am freer and more trusting.

I was the first woman hired in news at an ABC-TV station in Norfolk, Virginia. During my years at WVEC-TV, I had the opportunity to host a live daily television talk show, "Tidewater A.M." I interviewed hundreds of celebrities, politicians, and dignitaries. My most memorable interview was with Dr. Norman Vincent Peale, the author of *The Power of Positive Thinking* and many other well-known books. I am embarrassed to admit that during that stage in my life, Dr. Peale had little relevance for me. However, in my interview with him, he planted a seed in my mind. That idea began to sprout a few years ago, and now impacts my life, my work and, I am certain, the lives of many others. He suggested that when we are with people, especially strangers, we can recite an internal prayer, asking that those around us like us and that we like them. Liking or caring is a second important factor toward trust. Begin each experience with another person by finding something to like, respect, or care for.

Zaclon's Krimmel supported the risk-taking action of one of his people by giving personal and documented feedback in the form of a handwritten note.

"I sent the note to him on a Wednesday. I happened to see him again on Friday and he was carrying it. He pulled it out and said, 'Thank you, I appreciate it.' That really reinforced my use of this.

"Since then, I have done a similar thing with two of our marketing managers nailing down specific accounts on some long-term contracts. I still use the voice mail system and direct phone, but I think a written note, if it's not overdone, is most effective. My fear is that I will tend to overdo it. I don't want people to say, hey did you get one, I got one, did you get one? I want to try to save it for things that are more along the self-management line. I'll use the phone or verbal praise for other things. I am trying to use those cards for people taking initiative and going beyond their traditional jobs."

A conversation I had with Frank Mosier, a senior officer of an international oil company, stunned me. He reiterated what I had observed: that until recently, many business school textbooks taught management techniques that imprison the work force. The belief was very simple: people perform better when leadership is critical of them. It is no wonder people are uncomfortable with giving and receiving positive feedback!

The third factor toward building trust is open support and positive feedback for risk-taking action. This empowers people to continue risking.

This same oil company executive told a poignant story of another company that is no longer in existence. One easily sees why. The chairman insisted that there be required formal, restricted, labeled seating for executives during lunch. Seating was allowed only after the chairman rang a bell. This rigidity symbolizes our cultural addiction to control, power, and elitism—the very characteristics that have triggered the demise of the American spirit, halting change and freezing people into fear and mediocrity.

Mosier reiterated this fear with other compelling examples. After he had been CEO of a company, he realized that his successful past history dictated a thinking pattern of believing he knew what would or would not work, and that he was no smarter or more creative as a result. Thus, he provided an opportunity for labor, supervisors, and middle managers to put forth their ideas, knowing that these people were seldom asked for their opinions. He sought their thoughts by telling them that they had good ideas that were probably better or more effective than what they were already doing. The frontline people responded with an outpouring of ideas.

However, their managers and supervisors were defensive, creating a brick wall that buffered the creativity. Their fear, which is universal, is that the managers and supervisors do not want to look bad. In other words, they want to sell ideas "upward" as their own. Mosier contends this is demotivating. People need to be given credit for their ideas. Otherwise a company builds a lot of "yes-people"—people who do as little as they can, who don't go the extra mile because they do not get the credit for creativity.

Mosier referenced an article about the late William Paley, a CBS executive who was extraordinarily good at promoting the ideas of others as his own and giving no credit to the source. In fact, Mosier maintains that a company will have higher motivation and morale by giving people more credit than is deemed necessary. He contends that the other fear of middle managers and supervisors is that they worry they will be viewed as a barrier to progress—especially when ideas emerge from their people, as in the example Mosier gave, when they haven't been emerging right along. He also believes this problem exists with all layers of an organization.

Mosier states that most organizations need an overhaul. "People have been doing business in the same way for twenty years. They cannot change overnight. They succeeded because they understood how to use the organization for their success. To expect change is naive. Only twenty percent are flexible enough to adapt." He believes women will function better in future organizations because of their relationship skills, their ability to work cooperatively with people toward a solution, and their openness to diverse ideas when solving complex problems. People have fear because they have not been personally empowered, according to Mosier. They would not be filled with fear had they been personally empowered, nor would they be where they are today. Nor does fear work as a motivating factor. Fear is the weapon that is used in Iraq. It destroys. He concludes that the fear syndrome goes all the way to the top guy who worries about losing his fat salary.

"Fear is useless. What is needed is trust."

All we need to do is explore the dynamics of a family unit to see that past negatives can have the same toxic effect. I have been divorced for a number of years. As a single parent, I have been interested in giving forgiveness to and receiving forgiveness from my children. Much to my chagrin and dismay, I experienced a relationship with my son wherein he continued negative behavior even in light of my forgiveness and my introducing alternative coping skills. Finally, I realized that the same behavior I witnessed from him was also the same behavior I despised in his father. I hadn't "let go" of nor had I forgiven his father's behavior.

It was only when my son heard me say to his father with deep sincerity that I also forgave him and that I hoped he would learn other coping skills that I experienced relief. Brant's behavior changed; his father's behavior changed; and I stopped operating out of a past negative unforgiving self. Truly we build trust by role modeling the same message to all people in our life—not just some people some of the time. Forgiveness allows us to be free and let go of any negative past event, situation, or person.

A similar situation developed at the Fortune 500 company I worked with. The executive in charge made a blunder and said some very foolish things to his managers. After the negative impact of these hurtful remarks, he wished he had never said them. It was only after a sincere apology and willingness to be vulnerable that the team of managers could "let go" of the incident and move forward productively.

How many past negatives are we holding on to that dramatically interfere with performance, productivity, and trust? Those are the layers and layers of barriers that need to be erased and replaced with positive, encouraging, open relationships and communication.

First, we must forgive ourselves, and then forgive others. I recall attending a conference where we were instructed to go to total strangers and ask for forgiveness, not for our actions, but for the actions accomplished by uncaring people, who, in the past, had directly or indirectly lashed out and hurt them. Feeling vulnerable, uncomfortable, and fearful, I did as instructed. It was a powerful experience. I felt cleansed, whole, and forgiving. A forgiving heart heals, allowing release of the toxic fear barrier to trust, and causing a "letting go" of negative contaminants.

In Bright Side seminars, participants are asked to do something similar: to receive and give forgiveness. Even for the small things, it brings to mind the prayer of Saint Francis of Assisi:

O Lord,
Make me an instrument of your peace.
Where there is hatred, let me sow love;
Where there is injury, pardon;
Where there is doubt, faith;
Where there is despair, hope;
Where there is darkness, light;
Where there is sadness, joy.

O Divine Master,
Grant that I may not so much seek
To be consoled as to console,
To be understood as to understand,
To be loved as to love.
For it is in giving that we receive,
It is in pardoning that we are pardoned;
And it is in dying that we are born to eternal life.

In order to build trust, we must first trust ourselves. In order for that to flourish, a lot of internal healing is necessary.

Since we idealize our parents, it is understandable that we often minimize our childhood experiences. Yet it is those experiences that determine our ability to risk and be creative. Communicating feeling is a risky endeavor for us. No wonder—as children, we learned not to express our emotions.

On the other hand, loving inner dialogue makes us less critical and more receptive. Strong emotions fill our mind, create empowerment or imprisonment in our thinking and in our behavior. In today's highly competitive global market, people are worried and fearful. Those emotions reduce productivity and morale.

David Johnson, researcher and author, wrote: "A person without feelings is not a person at all; he or she is a machine. What we need more of has been suppressed, denied, deadened . . . the heart and spirit of people."

When we are vulnerable, we also build trust. We shed the masks of power, control, fear.

I was struck by the pure nakedness of personhood and unmasked emotion in a scene from the 1990 movie *Dances With Wolves*. In the movie the two main characters, Dances With Wolves and Stands With A Fist, are reunited. Without hesitation, they passionately greet each other, colliding and falling to the snow in deep, honest emotional expression. A powerful sense of intimate human love is revealed. They are utterly unencumbered.

Like them, we should be willing to let go of our defensive, disruptive, encumbering behavior.

I love my freedom to be who I am.	I respect your freedom to be who you are.
I love my right to be different from you.	I recognize your right to be different from me.
I can say yes.	You can say yes.
I can say no.	You can say no.
I am not responsible for you.	You are not responsible for me.
I want to be your sister.	You may be a brother with me.
I trust.	You trust.

We trust.

☆ *BRIGHT SIDE ENERGIZERS* ☆

- Today I will trisk by ____________________
- Today I will forgive myself by ____________________
- Today I will "let go" and forgive by ____________________
- Today I will build trust by ____________________
- Today I will become vulnerable by ____________________
- Today I will understand myself better; I will write about my deepest thoughts and emotions.
- Today I will share something that most people do not know about me.

Chapter Fourteen

The Dark Side

> You have been told also that life is darkness, and in your weariness you echo what was said by the weary.
> And I say that life is indeed darkness save when there is urge,
> And all urge is blind save when there is knowledge,
> And all knowledge is vain save when there is work,
> And all work is empty save when there is love;
> And when you work with love you bind yourself to yourself, and to one another, and to God.
>
> —Kahlil Gibran
> From *The Prophet*

An exceptionally successful, caring, and wealthy man was institutionalized, overwhelmed by the rage of his repressed anger. When he was a young man, he and his father had argued. When the man was thirty, his father, sixty, abandoned the family. He never came back. Some thirty years later, at the very same age, on the exact date, the son broke down, unable to function as those intense feelings began to erupt and emerge.

He was distanced from and numb to his feelings until they could no longer be contained. Perhaps he is a product of our culture, where the wounded inner child continues to contaminate our adult lives.

John Bradshaw maintains that all of us, to some extent, come from dysfunctional families, and that we carry within us a wounded inner child. This child is responsible for our violence and cruelty. It is the cause of our addictions, whether to substances, people, or activities.

The wounded inner child will dog us and interfere with our lives until we stop evading our pain. We often numb ourselves to feeling and pain by addiction. It is estimated that there are 131 million addicts in our society. The addictions falsely alter our moods, providing something that isn't.

The rules of our family systems are abusive. First, men have all of the power. Second, there is emotional repression as we erroneously learn that showing emotions is a sign of weakness. We are taught it is better not to feel, and that logic is superior to feeling and creativity.

I can remember, as a little girl, my mother correcting me. At seven, I insisted my father didn't love me. My mother, because of the rules she had been taught, corrected my inner truth—what I thought, felt, and saw. "Your father loves you. He doesn't call, write, or visit because I asked him not to. He certainly loves you," she said. What a destructive and confusing message! I learned not to believe or trust what I felt, thought, or experienced. I equated love with absence, abandonment, and abuse. The image I grasped was that of being hugged and stabbed at the same time.

Too often, our family rules prohibit us from expressing our hurt and anger. I was not allowed to verbally express my anger. Yet, my anger kept interfering. Enraged as a child, I took scissors to my wooden toy chest and gouged its surface. "Sweet girls don't do that," I was told. Enraged as an adult, I turned the volcanic anger inward, causing colitis and then a skin disorder. I rejected myself and married a man who called rejection and emotional abandonment "love." I imagined my then-husband injecting heroin in my arm. I knew something was amiss.

As we view John Bradshaw's wounded child questionnaires

and wounded child indexes of suspicion, we see that fear and mistrust issues reflect this woundedness.

Some of Bradshaw's indicators:

- Mistrust of people
- Fear of abandonment
- Fear of trying new experiences
- Fear of anger
- Fear of saying "no" directly
- Trouble identifying what you are feeling
- Difficulty in expressing your feelings
- Excessive competitiveness
- Intense fear of making a mistake

My continually acting out my anger interfered with my life until I began healing the wounded inner child that was my dark side, my inner Goliath.

Is this the same fear, lack of trust, and emotional numbness that is operating in today's corporate environment?

At Zaclon, when participants talked about experiences of being loved, one man said all of his memories were of violence and cruelty, being physically and verbally abused. According to Bradshaw, when we are not loved for the precious, tender prize we are, we develop a deep spiritual wound. We need unconditional love.

As an adult, that repeated pattern of anger kept showing itself in my life. A situation with my mother triggered the rage, pain, and abandonment of my childhood. In therapy, my inner child confronted that anger and lack of protection. In a subsequent session, my mother herself nurtured and loved that hurting inner Donna Rae. How blessed and fortunate I was to have my mother courageous enough to attend the session! It allowed the child frozen within by fear, hurt, and anger to be free of this toxic contamination.

In Bright Side sessions, I discovered that some people struggled to recall a positive childhood experience. That is why I encouraged participants to rediscover a past positive experience from any time period in their lives. What I now understand is that some people are so deeply wounded that it is hard to celebrate joyful childhood memories because so much feeling is toxic and repressed.

Yet, inside each of us, there is this delightful kid filled with wonder, resiliency, joy, courage, and adventure: our own unique being.

I was once given an article about ceramic cups that people used to cry into. In other words, cups to save your tears. The Hebrews kept two kinds of tear cups: one for when they were sad, and one for when they were happy. The fullness of the cups were reflections of the aliveness of people. The more tears in the cup, the fuller the cup, and the more that person was esteemed. Imagine, high esteem for people who are fully alive with emotion! For people who care and who are filled with passion and compassion! People who easily cry for joy! People who cry for pain!

We need to feel the full range of emotion in our lives and in our work. We need to care about the violence in our world. We need to become full alive to the pain and joy of our world. We must laugh and cry to show we are persons who care deeply, who are sensitive to ourselves and others.

Scientific research documents that crying and laughing are cleansing, ridding us of the toxic biochemicals produced by stress.

Many therapeutic programs have individuals hold dolls or stuffed animals to help access and unfreeze their deep inner feelings. Even though as children we are naturally trusting, we learned not to trust self. We were taught that what we felt, thought, saw, and said wasn't actually what we felt, thought, saw, or said. We were robbed of our sense of wonder, joy, love, play, feeling, and emotion. No wonder the corporate climate views love, play, and feeling as inappropriate! The dysfunction has been carried into the working world. How can the spirit of individuals and a team of employees be reawakened without feeling, without love and without fun?

Allison Roe sparked my own inner child. Knowing her, I could see my inner child blossom: adorable, courageous, worthy, deserving. Can you picture your own precious inner child, the beautiful child you once were? Can you nurture, accept, and love that being of wonder? Can we as managers and leaders facilitate nurturing of self and of others? Can we show people we love them as they are? Can we help reparent one another by reflecting each other's goodness and worthiness? Can we accept and cherish each other's differences, so that in our work we can fully celebrate and utilize individual uniqueness?

Experiences I have had with organizations clearly show that a team can surpass individual performance. Can you imagine how much more powerful and effective teams would be if people were empowered to be exactly who they are? The negative use of energy to repress self and emotion is then available for much greater individual and team purposes and for our creative wonder. We are no longer focused on ''What's wrong with me'' but on a sense of doing our unique creative work.

We have been taught that logic is superior, and to be logical one must deny feelings. Nothing is further from the truth. Feelings are energy. Denying feelings can distort our behavior and judgment, darkly coloring our perceptions. That is the dark side: crippling and distorting us and our relationships.

Each May, Revco Inc. hosts a marathon and 10K race in Cleveland. Thousands of people compete. While running the Revco 10K, I was awed by wheelchair participants. As each one passed, my heart swelled with excitement and tenderness. Many of us cheered and applauded their courageousness. Overwhelmed by the intensity of my inner feeling, I realized that we were each applauding and cheering our own wounded inner being. That inner child, emotionally crippled because he/she had never been emotionally or spiritually validated, still waited for some sign of encouragement—the standing ovation, the positive regard that says "Come forth! You are welcome!"

☆ *BRIGHT SIDE ENERGIZER* ☆

List all of the warm welcoming statements you can provide yourself and others.

____

____

____

I will cry tears of joy and loss.
I will applaud myself.
I will applaud others.
I will acknowledge my inner child.

Chapter Fifteen

Transforming

It is a funny thing about life; if you refuse to accept anything but the best, you very often get it.

—W. Somerset Maugham
From *The Mixture as Before*

It is revitalizing to attend classes that provide new learning. At Bright Side, each Tuesday we attend an international Bible study program. It is a renewing experience for me and my staff. It often amazes me to what great extent many of our enriching values and principles are based on the Bible and how few of us know the source of this enrichment.

At Bright Side, we believe ongoing learning is an essential part of growth and change. Each day each of us can learn something new. I introduced the starpower concept at the Inc. 500 Conference. Starpower is really the embodiment of the principle that each of us has an underlying need to be validated, appreciated, valued, and loved. After asking Bright Side participants about the last time they received a gold star, they are then encouraged to give and receive positive feedback, and in the process to keep record of their energy level and mood states.

Participants are sometimes uncomfortable with being positive about themselves, giving positive feedback, and receiving positive feedback. This is not surprising, for many of us have had more experiences with negative or critical feedback. For example, Jesuit psychologist John Powell in *Happiness Is an Inside Job* documents that many of us up until the age of five have received over an average of four hundred comments daily that are limiting, negative, or critical. This, along with many other ''ought-to'' statements, has shaped us, conditioned us, formed us. John Bradshaw maintains that we may have as much as twenty-five thousand hours of critical parenting. If there is one area we can change, it is the learning that we have internalized.

The negative learning statements can be transformed into positive learning statements.

It is helpful to visualize the mind as a gray kneaded putty that can be shaped, stretched, and formed with new input. This piece of putty is in fact a tool to help us change from a negative thought pattern to a positive thought pattern. We can, in fact, erase the negative and begin fresh and new each day with joyful, awesome, loving, affirming statements:

- I am unworthy *to* I am worthy.
- I am unlovable *to* I am lovable.
- I am of little value *to* I am valuable.
- I am insignificant *to* I am awesome.
- I am guilty *to* I am free of guilt.
- I bear grudges *to* I forgive myself and others.
- I fill with the negative *to* I let go of the negative and fill with the positive.
- I live on the dark side *to* I live on the Bright Side.

Living on the Bright Side encompasses transforming negative thinking to positive thinking; to hearing and receiving within our heart the positive feedback that we so often reject. We reject compliments by the barriers of darkness surrounding us that we have built up as children, deflecting goodness. It is the giant Goliath, the garbage thinking, that we have made so powerful. It is also through self-indulgence that we become slaves to a negative addiction that is harmful to our well-being.

In attending one of our Bible study sessions, the leader spoke of her own inability and immaturity in accepting positive feedback. She shared how one of her friends suggested opening the top of her shirt to let in a positive remark, and to allow it to nurture her by gently patting it as it entered through this opening. I chuckled. How clever a suggestion!

As we left this session, Janeen spoke to me and then playfully pulled open the top of my shirt to let in the compliment she had just given to me, one that I had not even heard! That validates that we teach that which we also need . . . I had not even heard her words of encouragement, the armor of negativity was so strong that morning. I took on a deeper realization that there are times that we not only consciously reject or question goodness, but that we also can be numb to letting goodness in because of the numbness we have developed to protect ourselves from hurt or pain.

Receiving compliments is comparable to receiving love. It takes practice. Today, record each compliment you receive by opening the top of your shirt to ensure that you receive it fully and completely into your heart. It is childish and immature to not fully receive compliments. Our society has conditioned us to perhaps think the opposite: that it is childish and immature to place much importance and basic goodness on ourselves and others. When we think we are unable to change, we destroy our peace of mind, dignity, and self-respect.

Begin each day triumphantly and victoriously, working on renewing the mind by stretching out of the comfort zone of doubt, fear, negative feedback, and by creating a new, joyful, world open to encouragement, coaching, and positive feedback.

God has a real purpose for each and every tender life. It is when we are able to step out of the darkness of destructive habits and into the light of God's word that we begin to achieve clarity as to our reason for being.

The following heartwarmers were compiled by Helen Lesmar:

"Grant me the wisdom, Oh Lord, to know that sharing does not mean losing."

"Instill in me, Oh Lord, a caring heart for it is in caring and sharing that my life is enriched and my joys are multiplied."

When I was asked to speak at the Inc. 500 Conference honoring America's fastest growing privately held corporations, I felt a mixture of blood-pushing excitement and nerve-racking fear. Certainly, if there was an audience that was highly motivated, that would be the one. It could also be my most sophisticated and challenging audience.

The morning that I was to travel to Raleigh, North Carolina, there were heavy thunderstorms in Cleveland. It was not the kind of weather I enjoy traveling in. As I prepared to leave for my office, I received a shocking phone call from the dry cleaner. They could not locate the suit I was to wear for my presentation! I became very frustrated, and I had to remind myself that I was supposed to be the expert on positive-motivation and releasing stress. I was promised that they would try to find the one-of-a-kind suit.

One hour prior to leaving for Raleigh, the dry cleaner telephoned once again. They found my suit—but it was still dirty. But they promised to get it cleaned in one hour. Frazzled, to say the least, I drove through heavy traffic to get my precious presentation suit. Deep relaxation breathing couldn't begin to wash away the mounting tension and the anxiety that was enveloping me.

Arriving at the airport with not a moment to spare, I decided to park in the garage for easier and quicker access into the airport terminal. I became more anxious. I could not find a parking space. All I observed were signs warning of falling concrete due to construction. After what seemed an endless search for a parking space, one was found. I raced off to the terminal.

For the first time in my life, airport security stopped me. They wanted to inspect my briefcase. Rough hands pulled out all contents, only to discover a crucifix my sister had given to me. I wondered how a crucifix could be confused with a dangerous weapon. However, I quickly dismissed the thought, realizing how great the fear is that has been instilled in people of our culture. Nonetheless, I was cleared, deemed harmless, and very rapidly walked to my gate.

Once I arrived at my gate, at the far end of the terminal, I was struck by the absence of other passengers. The plane has been delayed, I was told. I took in a breath of relief. At least I had enough time to go to the bathroom.

Heading toward the lavatory signs, I went in to the stall. Just as I was ready to open the stall door to leave, I gasped. There, before my very eyes, was a man with his back to me using the urinal. What am I going to do? I worried. I can't stay in the bathroom all day. My anxiety level soared. Every muscle in my body tensed with fear and embarrassment. I didn't want this man or any other man to see me in the men's bathroom.

I slouched back in the corner of the stall sulking and feeling sorry for myself. Then, I heard a zipping sound. It was the zipping sound of this man zipping up his pants that triggered the five-year-old that lives within me. I got the deep inner giggles. I kept the giggling down deep inside of me. It felt good, like bubbles of happiness, bursting in my body. All of my worries and anxiety swept gallantly away, but I forced my giggles to soften. I did not want the man to know I had watched him use the urinal.

It was when I internally laughed that I could feel all of my tension vanish. Whoever said laughter is the best medicine knew exactly what he or she was talking about.

I was holding back outrageous laughter when this man proceeded to stand right in front of my stall (at the sink) to make final bathroom preparations: washing hands, combing hair, and *unzipping his pants* to tuck in his shirt (of course)! That was all I needed to see. The silent giggles became loud uproaring laughter. I burst out of the stall profusely apologizing—mixed with the laughter that bellowed forth.

"Oh, I am so sorry," I managed to apologize amidst the fits of laughter. By stark contrast, he didn't see anything funny. The look on his face told me he didn't believe me.

I knew I had to get out of there before I encountered another man. I spun myself immediately around and there, standing right in front of me, was one of the most handsome men I had ever seen, laughing at *me*! What a relief, I thought. At least this one is laughing. He proceeded to talk to me—right there in the men's bathroom. He told me he heard me when I first came in, that he had been in the stall next to me. He thought he was the one who had made the mistake! We roared together. As we were preparing to leave the men's room together, laughing, almost arm-in-arm, in walked another woman entering the men's bathroom! (Obviously she had seen *me* enter and had thought it was the women's bathroom!)

Laughter, called "internal jogging" by Norman Cousins, is a simple and playful way to break tension and to release that highly optimistic, enthusiastic, wonderful kid that lives inside all of us. Laughter and humor may be our greatest coping mechanisms. (And when used in the men's bathroom, I have learned it is the best way to meet good-looking men!)

After attending a Bright Side series of seminars, a foreman explained that using laughter felt like a Bright Side booster. At an

IBM meeting, Gregg Searle asked his people to come up with a laughter quota. At a national meeting of a major real estate development company, attendees were asked to laugh for no reason at all. The next day, many of them confided that they laughed just to laugh while driving—and even that made a difference in their attitude and how they felt.

At Loma Linda University, Dr. Lee Berk has researched the effect of laughter and humor on the human body. Although it is inconclusive as to whether endorphins (natural mood-elevating biochemicals) are increased, Dr. Berk did find that laughter and humor may reduce the toxic biochemicals produced by stress.

There is one major American sentiment that blocks the belief that relaxing, playful attitudes bring us to a peak performance state. In our culture, we have learned that work is serious and that peak performance comes from seriousness and intensity.

To understand the concept, think of athletes preparing for peak performance. It is common to see them in loose, relaxed, and playful behavior to reduce pre-performance stress. Think of your own performances. They are enhanced when you are relaxed and joyful compared to when you are serious and intense. In fact, it is easy to feel the tension strangling our ability to think clearly or creatively. One philosopher wrote that playfulness may be the only ingredient necessary for creativity. Albert Einstein wrote about free play with concepts. It is the child within that helps us unlock our rich inner treasure of individual talent and thinking. I recall watching the Winter Olympics—and my favorite sport—ice skating. The Canadian competitor, Elizabeth Manley, who publicly stated that she went through therapy to learn to skate for the pure joy, received the silver medal; while American competitor, Debi Thomas, was overly intense and serious, to the point where negative self-talk and repeated stumbling cost her the gold.

Building spirit, a sense of joy and fun, is paramount to accessing individual and team potential. The ability to play with ideas to find solutions often appears silly, yet allows us to feel comfortable with even the most outlandish idea our imagination can generate.

Out of many weird or unusual ideas, we find a new solution to an old problem. We can't ask people to have fun only occasionally, it is like asking people for occasional excellence. We must be in the habit of fun for it to work for us.

Progressive Insurance Company, one of America's most profitable companies, asked me to travel nationwide to bring the message of fun, love, spirit, and play to their employees. The resulting positive energy proves how people are looking for joy. How do we change habits of a lifetime—the habits that we learned as children—to cope with everyday anxiety? We must be willing to grow and change.

☆ *BRIGHT SIDE ENERGIZERS* ☆

- Recall a time when you think you were very funny.
- Establish your own laugh quota. Laugh a minimum of six times daily. Deep belly laughs!
- Give and receive starpower. When you are given positive regard, open your shirt at the neck to fully and completely receive it.
- Laugh, heartily, for no reason!
- Draw a cartoon of your funny self—your "humor hero."
- Transform a negative into a positive! Discover a "laugh" in the midst of tension!
- Mentally picture your "peak performance" self.

• *Starpower*

I introduced the starpower concept at the 1989 Inc. 500 Conference, honoring the CEOs of America's fastest-growing companies. Since starpower's introduction, I have encouraged Bright Side seminar participants to think of other ways to use this concept of positive feedback for increased trust and positive relationships. Each day for one week I encourage you to think of three new ways to give positive feedback. Then commit to at least one of them.

To stimulate your creativity for generating new ideas for positive feedback, I offer you the following Bright Side starpower ideas.

- Bring the stars to a meeting and hand them out to each person in attendance, after giving each person encouragement and positive feedback.

- For one day, find a positive alternative with every person or situation and give yourself a star.
- Give recognition to team members for creative, positive, or risk-taking action by giving away stars.
- Send an uplifting quote to inspire your team members. Include a star. "Reach high, for stars lie hidden in your soul. Dream deep, for every dream precedes the goal." (Pamela Vaull Starr)
- Find a positive way to respond to even the most challenging situation. Give yourself a star.

In place of stars, you may want to try a standing ovation or the Awesome concept.

Remember . . . what's important is you!

Chapter Sixteen

The Bright Side Can Work

An Interview with Jack Kahl
President and CEO
Manco, Inc.

> You need numbers. But I don't make decisions from the numbers.
>
> —Jack Kahl

Jack Kahl, Jr., president and CEO of Manco, Inc., began his tenure with the company in 1963. In 1966 he became general manager, and on June 1, 1971, he purchased the business.

When Kahl joined the firm in 1963, annual sales totaled $83,000. Under his leadership sales grew to $5 million in 1978 and are expected to reach $70 million in 1991.

Manco is a consumer market vendor of weatherstripping, mailing supplies, and Duck brand adhesive tape. Manco's trademark is a colorful family of Manco ducks.

The theme of the cuddly and colorful Manco family of ducks is evident throughout Manco: Spirit (How High Can We Climb) awards; greeting cards for all seasons and holidays; the Manco Duck Costume Character; Manco plush Duck dolls and toys; Manco Ducktails Newsletter; the Manco Duck Challenge Swim and even signs of ducks on machines, towmotors, and throughout Manco offices.

In this chapter, Kahl talks about how his childhood shaped his life and how he empowers his employees to achieve.

DS: Hi! How come you look so good?

JK: It's the Christmas season. I got a lot done today. Just before you got here, I was sitting here with my eyes closed, catching my Chinese nap and trying to slow the motor down from 100 to 95.

You know we're in retail. Retail is hurting. People are smashing and burning their prices in the markups. This has been the toughest Christmas in twenty-seven years.

We are here to serve our customers. This is their busiest time of year. The whole focus of our company has to be here to serve.

DS: What is it they might need from you?

JK: Help, answers, service. The retailers may want to place an order. They may want to call in here to get inventories updated. They may want to cancel an order, which they have been busy doing lately because business is terrible. Our business is good, but their business is not.

DS: How could your business be good and theirs not?

JK: Because the niches that we are in are profitable and growing: for us, mailings, supplies, tape, which people hold their world together with, tape at a buck to two dollars a roll. But winter coats, durable goods, and other things that fit in great big stores that we don't have to worry about selling, they do. People aren't spending money. They are holding on tight. Old folks like you and me. Two-thirds of the wealth of this country is in the hands of people of fifty and up. The country keeps getting older and older and the yuppies in the twenty-five to forty age group are fast dwindling in numbers. So those who have the money are getting older, and they are more demanding, more persnickety, and so the whole psychographics of spending is changing as a result of age groups.

Now the mentality is fear. Fifty-year-old people remember bad times. They've heard it from their parents, and they've been through enough recessions. I've been through them, because I'm fifty. So I remember. I know what's going on, and I'm not spending a lot this year. I'm going out tonight and buying one good-quality thing for each one of my kids: one good, lasting, quality gift.

I had my Christmas today. I just wrote letters and sent checks to foundations—I like myself a lot right now. I also sent a check to a woman who lost her husband, killed in a fire, who worked here. She is probably the most needful one of all. I've given to her, her little kids. She was at our Christmas party with her eight-year-old boy who was in the fire (she lost one boy in the fire). He was there in a burn suit all the way up to his neck, but I didn't see it because it was under his things.

He put out his little hand. He couldn't shake hands with his right hand, so I had to shake his left hand. And I'm thinking, whoa boy, what a year this little guy had, and you wouldn't know it! He was smiling and happy even though he had burn scars all over the side of his face. Yet, he was at the party, he had seen Santa Claus and he was happy.

His mother is out of a job and needed help, so the Manco people collected money that they usually use to give me a gift, and they gave her a gift certificate for Christmas, $270. We didn't make any big announcement. We just invited her quietly and gave her the money. She stuck around at the end to thank me and introduce me to her two kids, so I met this little Jimmy. I was quite taken by his courage, and the smile that he kept through everything.

We're looking to see if we can find a job for her here. In the meantime, she needs a Christmas. I was once in that kind of position, a long time ago.

DS: What happened to you?

JK: When we were kids in Cleveland, we were on welfare, so Christmas was somebody else's hand-me-downs wrapped up, which was fine. At the time it was great. Had it not been for education, my father's hard work, and my desire to improve, I still might be down on West Twenty-fifth Street where she lives.

I think back a lot of times, had I not gotten out of there and not gotten out to apple orchards and pear orchards and a better neighborhood, there's no telling where I would have gone. Two of my buddies were both dead before they were eighteen years old. We weren't bad guys, but we were hanging around with people in a bad environment.

I was a mischievous youngster. I'm always taking chances. When I was 10, I was in a gang. My brother and I were the leaders. We had Puerto Rican buddies, all kinds of great buddies. We would shake the bums under the High Level bridge, wake them up, make them chase us, do all kinds of things. Occasionally, we would break into an old condemned building just to see what was in there.

DS: I didn't know of this!

JK: My dad had TB. Only rest was prescribed then, so he spent a lot of time in the hospital. My recollection of my father early on was seeing him from a fourth-story window. He would throw money from a coin purse, which he shouldn't even have done. Everything was contamination, and they didn't understand TB so they put him in a sanatorium. He had TB three times, for a year, year and a half, and year and a half. The third time they perfected an operation called lobectomy, which was cutting out the diseased part of the lung. That finally did cure him.

During that time we went from the old neighborhood where my parents grew up, to tough times, the West Twenty-fifth Street projects and welfare for my mother. A lot of relatives looked down on us, and made us feel less than good. I remember those things. But some wonderful relatives always brought potatoes and ice cream and took me to the circus and made me feel good about myself.

My mom was a jewel. She said as the oldest boy, I needed a

job. We needed money. I was seven. I was sled riding one day and I saw this guy with a paper route. I knocked on his window. And he said, what do you want, kid? And I said mister, I want a job. How old are you? he asked. I told him and he said, why do you want a job? I told him.

He said, well, you go around the projects and if you can find any people who will take the paper, I'll give you a route. So I went all over, knocking on doors, and I found an old lady on the fourth floor who said she wanted a subscription. Then I went to the Harbor Inn Bar, which is still in business, where all the sailors used to come from all around the world. So the guy gave me a paper route with two customers.

I kept it for about two years. When I left two years later, I had twenty-two customers.

I swear my wanderlust started then. I used to go down to the bar and drop that paper off at the Harbor Inn. The sailors would put me up on the bar stool and they would talk, kid around, and buy me a pop, and I would hear these guys talk with different languages and I was always taken by it. I always wanted to know more. I liked it. They were real kind to me. My whole impression of the world was made first by these people.

Then I would leave and go in the projects. Big guys intimidated us little ones. You are rated by how tough you are. We were starting to see a lot of minorities, blacks and Puerto Ricans, moving into the projects. My brother and I were becoming leaders of the pack. My mom was always worried about us because my dad wasn't there. She couldn't control all the kids all the time. So that was my early background.

Then my dad came home. He worked for American Greetings Corporation, as Irving Stone's secretary (Irving Stone is the chairman and founder of American Greetings). He was extremely talented. He could write anything, almost on the spot. He's that talented.

So anyway, he started making comments because Irving had to approve every verse. When he went into meetings and read them, my father went along to take notes. My father started making comments and adding verse. Before you knew it, my father was checking verses. Then he was working in the verse department. Before you knew it, my father was the head of the verse department!

My dad finally made enough money. He got in real estate at night part-time and started making more money. He couldn't get his boss to give him a big enough raise, so he did another thing which I admire him for: he quit. We had six kids living in the projects and we were off welfare, but still very poor. Yet, he left that job. I'll never forget that. He went on straight commission in real estate to sell full time because he was making more money part time at nights and weekends than he was at American Greetings.

He never stopped. He worked his tail off seven days a week, and educated six kids. He got enough to buy our first house out near the airport, with apple orchards and woods. It cost $9,500. The garage fell down two months after we moved in. It had an old brick driveway, old-fashioned sink, and glass-covered doors, but every rug had a throw rug over it because there was a hole underneath it. My mother cried for three months when she moved in. She wanted to move back to the projects. It was a terrible house. But we kids loved it. We had polliwog ponds in the backyard. We put in a driveway and a new garage.

When we did move in, my dad worked too hard, and [that's when] he got TB for the third time. As soon as he would work hard physically he would tire out and get sick again. He went back to the hospital.

By that time I was now working two jobs and going to school. My brother and sister were working, too. My mother always gave us our own bank account. She always said this was our money and gave us credit for what we did. If she needed something, we'd go to the bank and get some money because the family needed it. We also had people who were great friends, who weren't even relatives but whom we called uncles and aunts, who just came over and helped. Those people taught me real generosity. At Christmastime—I really recall that. The root system of all this came from my mother, my father, and family.

DS: What you just described helped make you who you are today.

JK: What I just described gave me desire, a sense of achievement, and the recognition that comes from work. I always had a buck in my pocket. I always had a nickel. When I was on construction, I always put 80 percent of the money in the bank. Twenty percent was always enough to have a tank of gas. I had a car when I was sixteen, it was an old beat-up car, but it was mine. I always had control of myself and my environment. Work has given me a lot.

Also, I've gotten a lot of my shyness from a tough father, who expected good grades and had very strict standards. At times, he could be so expecting, so demanding, it made me shy because it took away my willingness to risk certain things. I had to overcome that in this business.

Part of the reason I started a small and manageable business was to get out of the limelight of downtown Cleveland, where I worked for one year and which I didn't like. Then I discovered Manco, built it, and got used to it. As it started getting bigger than what I thought I could manage, I was almost reverting back to days when I was a child, afraid that I couldn't handle what was coming. Business was going to grow, but it was going to grow past me and I was going to have to get out of this chair because I didn't think I had the personality to handle the job. I started reading books on it and started first pretending to others that I was capable of it but inside not believing. Now it's easy to share because now I know I can do it. But one time, in 1981, I didn't think so, I was Phineas T. Bluster from Howdy Dowdy. I was looking like it, talking like it, acting like it, but I didn't believe it for a minute.

DS: What caused you to believe?

JK: Falling flat on my back when I was out running around, selling and marketing and coming up with ideas and having a good time and risking everything. Owing the bank about $4 million, signed personally, and feeling in reasonably good control because I had people around me who I thought were in control as well. My downfall came in the least suspecting place, a fine young guy who was a brilliant finance man but was a terrible delegator. He couldn't delegate, but I didn't know it. He had four people under him, but he was falling further and further behind. One night he was just green-gray with anxiety. In front of all the other young people, he resigned, and told me why: the books were six months in arrears. He was completely befuddled and buried in work, way out of control financially.

It was a total shock. My whole security system, my family security system—everything—was endangered. I panicked, but not in front of people. I calmed them down. Then I got into a car that was two weeks old, that they encouraged me to get because it was my dream car. It was the first time I ever bought a car that I'd always dreamed of having. I hated driving it home. By the time I got home, I saw this brick house I lived in falling down. I thought I was having a nervous breakdown.

I was on my back for four weeks. I went to work, but I was completely broken in spirit because I was out of control and I thought I had bankrupted. It was far worse in my mind than it was in reality. I wasn't mad at the young guy. I held myself responsible for being so stupid that I had not seen it coming. It was the darkest single moment of my existence.

I lost a great deal of confidence in myself and my judgment. I got some counseling and found out a lot of people go through what I did. Slowly, ever so slowly, I started rebuilding a little faith in myself.

Nobody here knew how deep it went. Everybody knew I was tired and exhausted, but nobody knew how psychologically frightened I had been. I was taking anxiety pills mostly because I lacked faith in my own self-control and my own feelings. That went on for two years, 1981 to 1983. That was something. But that stuff teaches you a lot. I went out and started getting real smart people. What I had done is hire real young people. It was building the whiz kids and was getting great advice. The need to bring in people from professional service areas who could see the big picture became obvious to me. So I went and got Arthur Andersen and Calfee Halter and started to pay for what I wanted. I had to break relationships to do that. I had to ask others to step aside and act as advisers rather than doers. I kept the friendships, but changed the people who did the business. So there was a lot of emotional stuff going on. It changed me.

DS: How did you change?

JK: I did it through reading and mostly trying, and not quitting. That was the biggest thing.

DS: Tell me about standing alone to do the Wal-Mart cheer.

JK: Yes, I attended the shareholders meeting, down in the Arkansas field house. It was extraordinary. The following morning, I went to the Saturday morning meeting, and I was sitting in the audience with about nine hundred people—among them Wal-Mart associates and Wall Street financial analysts.

Sam Walton was in better style than ever because he was entertaining the Wall Street group. Saturday morning meetings are fun, but this one was extraordinary fun while getting the job done too. It's just that it was Barnum and Bailey time. It was so much fun and so uplifting, and I got so motivated sitting there that when David Glass, the president, asked if anybody had any questions, I raised my hand. I said, I don't have a question, I have to tell you something. Before you knew it, I was up the aisle, on stage, talking and telling all the Wal-Mart people what I thought of them, how much fun it was to come down there and work and share time with them. I said, you don't have to hear this because you know you're good, but I want you to know it anyway. I said I want to fulfill the dream that I have always had. I said, "I want to lead you guys in a Wal-Mart cheer," and so I did. Sam Walton said, well, let's give him some help. So he got the fourteen regional managers out of the front row, put them behind me and we started doing it. I forgot the hyphen of Wal-Mart. It's a squiggly, sort of wiggle and squiggle down to the knees. I didn't do it. They said, well, we'll have to get you down here again and teach you how to do a squiggly.

That was the first time in my entire life that I ever got up in front of a big group of people like that, and did something like that. I had thought about doing it hundreds of times but I never did. I never had the guts to do it. And now I see why other people don't do it—because they don't have the guts to do it.

When I get invited to do public speaking, even now, the first tendency, most of the time, is to refuse. I'm not a professional speaker. I'm not comfortable doing it, even though I like to talk about what I do. So my little battle with myself to keep improving is to not say no. I'll say no if I don't have time, but if I want to do it and it's a good cause, I say yes. It's more than just to tell the Manco story. It's to develop myself, not chicken out on myself.

DS: Sam Walton does jumping jacks and that kind of thing?

JK: He'll get in the middle of an hour-long meeting on Saturday morning. Everybody's sitting too still, so he'll say, come on now, let's get up, and suddenly you are doing jumping jacks right in your seat! Then we sit down. He runs you like a military drill instructor. Get up, sit down, do this, do that. He's in charge. And everyone is having a good time.

DS: Why did you do the Wal-Mart cheer?

JK: I was motivated to go beyond myself! Isn't it an amazing thing? It breaks through the fear. You break it by doing it. There's a sign back at Manco from Joseph Conrad. Everyone around here knows it's one of my top favorites. It says, "Facing up to your worst fears is the best thing that you can do. Look at it, deal with it."

DS: When you were a kid, did you make a conscious decision to have the gang leadership?

JK: It wasn't really a gang. It was a good group of kids who were starting to get into some pretty good mischief.

DS: Were you consciously aware of what was happening?

JK: No. All I can tell you is environment was creating that. We were looking for things to do. There was an empty building, and we decided to break a window and see what's in there. We found old pieces of glass that nobody wanted. We took them home. Mom beat the heck out of me and told me to take that back. She was frightened to death. Then I knew it was wrong. We didn't know at that time that what we did was wrong. We were afraid to take the glass back for fear we'd be in real trouble, so we threw it in the bushes somewhere.

DS: How did you go from that direction to where you are?

JK: I just went the Catholic school system and its tight structure. We moved to a whole different healthy environment with more money, baseball, and football instead of breaking into buildings.

But I was always a rebel. My dad and I clashed when I was a teenager, as most teens do. We disagreed on things. Then, when I was sixteen, I got a job working in construction. I grew muscles and a wallet that had money. Neighbors weren't making the kind of money I was making as a summer laborer! I bought a car for one hundred and fifty dollars. I had wheels, independence, money in my pocket, money in the bank I saved for school. And when we needed that money, my mother spent it, and yet there always was enough left that I was always feeling pretty good about it myself. Looking back, from seven years on, I had a job, and it gave me recognition and identity. I was given credit by my family for my work. The whole idea of working is a good thing. With me it was an environmental thing that came from family need, and a fantastic feeling, like being a thoroughbred at what you are able to do to contribute to the wellness of the family.

DS: How do you motivate your people?

JK: With open information, straightforward talk and communication. For example, we had a twenty-one-year-old kid here. They were going to let him go because he was always tardy. I learned he had a paper route in the morning. That's why he was tardy. Plus they were always yelling at him, not praising him. We made some changes.

We took the most people-oriented people we had and put them in charge of managing people. We took the technical people who were good with machines and put them in charge of machines.

This is an extraordinary young guy. He is a high school grad. He has two hundred *Plain Dealer* customers and he comes to work here, sets up the machine, and he runs it. He has a helper who puts stuff in the boxes for him. Scotty hung a quality-standard sign over the machine with all the eight things that can be wrong with the quality roll of gift wrap. He named each one, so that the people working the machine could immediately see if anything was wrong. It also shows them where to put rejects. He has a picture of the Manco Duck he drew on a piece of corrugated paper saying we "gotta take care of our customers." He did all that on his own. I went to his supervisor and told him this kid has talent to be supervisor in two years or less if only he wants to be. The kid has a heart as big as all outdoors. He's genuine, and he's smart, but he just doesn't believe in himself. He doesn't want to grow up and he's afraid, too. He talks too fast. But the kid has talent!

I want to help him. I told him, tell me what you want to do with your life and I'll try to help you get there. But you have to know first.

He says, what do you think I can do? I said, what do you want to be?

A poem about goals Scott Stefka wrote, well, he didn't know it, but I framed it and presented three framed copies to him: one for the wall of my office, one for his home, and one for the Manco wall of fame.

I told him, "Someone always has to believe in you. I see myself in you, and I want to step up and help you." That conversation was the best part of my day! I really believe in him and want to help him. I told him, "You can go as far as you want to go once you make up your mind. But first you have to know where you want to go." I told him to look at our plant manager. He only has a high school education! He started out as a beverage store manager; he started here part-time. But look how far he's come! I told Scott he'd make a great role model.

Also, I told him to look at Wal-Mart executive Dean Sanders. He's a high school graduate, too, but he'll probably be Wal-Mart president or CEO one day.

Scott attends our Thursday meetings by choice. I told him he can go as far as he wants to go; he just has to decide how far. Then I'll help him. So he's going to go home this weekend and start thinking about it.

DS: When you recognized his contribution, you really showed that he had a treasure that you appreciated and valued. Moving on, what about the meetings? How did you get that idea?

JK: It came from seeing the success of the Wal-Mart Saturday morning meetings. It is the value of the communication, the upbeat Sam Walton energy and fun, with cheers, jumping jacks, running in place, group activities, and togetherness. Sam Walton keeps their blood running and minds alert with cheers and fun yet with everyone's attention focused on the subject. He breaks tension in the middle of a long meeting, gets the blood running, the mind open and provides a seventh-inning stretch.

The real guts of what I saw was the total communication that never gets done between nine and five because nobody ever has time to get that many people together, so Saturday mornings became important to them. I started because I had an even bigger problem in our size company than he had in his. We could not get communication channeled through to other people fast enough at the rate of change in the marketplace. So I announced that we would have a Saturday morning meeting.

It was negatively received until the first meeting. It's been positive from that day on. People liked it. They discovered friends in other departments. All kinds of social bonds formed that never broke, and a lot of things took over that I'm sure are not in other companies because other companies don't do it.

DS: How does the meeting work?

JK: At first, the outside salesmen would come in. They would tell what they had learned this week in their territories about customers' competition, prices, new ideas, innovation, everything. Sitting in our group would be secretaries, operations people, finance people, and everybody. What I found was that we had focused too much on salesmen and sales. We had taken the inside people and made them feel a little subservient. I met Peter Drucker in 1980 and he said, remember, here's how to run a business. Buy cheap, package well, and sell dear. And that I remembered.

So our meeting starts with *sell dear*. We go back to the salesmen, then we go back to *buy cheap*, which means buying, and we have the operations and purchasing people give a report on raw materials. *Package well* is the marketing people. So the merchandising/marketing presentations are made. Afterwards, young guys sometimes go out for a few beers, and rookies are invited to join them. People bond, friendships are made, a beer or two is had, and the company keeps getting tighter. That's how it works.

DS: What do you think you do that makes the bonds?

JK: It's not me. It's everybody. It's openness, information, feedback, and willingness to try to find and celebrate the positive. Celebrate the positive and then that allows you to go after the negative in a fast-changing business.

DS: I find there is a lot of negativity out there—that garbage thinking that we talked about. It's Goliath. And the tools of love, fun, creativity, and feeling, that's David.

JK: That's what people don't and won't risk, especially in a man's world. They don't and won't risk their feelings and their hearts. I call it parking your heart at the curb. Most of them are parking their hearts in their parking lot. Then they come in, in a brusque businesslike face, gray-flannel-suit mind. They walk in and give you analytical fluff up to your ears. They give you another number, and talk head count talk, say we have to cut heads. That's an easy way to distance yourself, cut heads, use big-man talk. I don't want head talk in this company. There is a fear that comes into me because this is the Manco family. The fear that gets me pretty intense at times is driven by not wanting to have to face letting people go. There's no need for letting people go if you do things right.

DS: But it is a very positive environment. I wish everybody could see what you have here, because it succeeds. It takes your role modeling for that positive, open environment to exist.

JK: We have summer concerts, we bring hospital speakers in to help with stress. We improved the weight room. We offer college reimbursement, new office furniture, family things: Cleveland Indians special family day, kids' coloring contests, smoke alarms, Christmas party, Thanksgiving turkey. For the

Earth Day celebration, we all took home potted plants. We added park benches around our pond. We recycle in our plants. We planted trees on Arbor Day and sent everyone home with a tree. We have annual summer concerts around the Manco ponds featuring the Singing Angels. We operate as a family. We have Santa Claus visit us at our annual Christmas party. We are an ESOP (Employee Stock Ownership Plant) which makes every single person a partner and owner in the Manco family. We share the risks and we share the rewards.

Also, every year we have a lottery. I give $500 of my own money to the person who comes closest to guessing the year's total sales figures.

Then I had a contest. We had a problem. We needed to reduce our inventory. Many times people are afraid to discuss problems, but I wanted to humanize the problem and make fun of it so that people were not afraid to bring it up. So I had a contest to see who could come up with the most clever way to name this problem so we could deal with it.

The winner was a young man who had just become a new father. His mother works here, too. He nicknamed the inventory-control problem SCUD, or ''Still Collecting Unwanted Dust.'' Isn't that great? I really liked his creativity! I gave him $200 from my own pocket for that, too.

We also have a bell that we ring whenever there's good news. I think that helps employee morale, too. The bell is also rung when I talk too much at a meeting.

With the Manco Duck, well, people asked to have duck symbols and signs for their own decoration and it just spread. I love it. It's like a barometer, and if people want to display it, it means they like the place. To me, it says they're giving their heart and souls to this place. It's also a sign of warmth and fun, almost like a Walt Disney atmosphere! A Manco rep carries a plush Manco

Duck doll in his car. This same man is receiving the Spirit Award for energizing a client meeting with the Manco cheer.

Work needs to be fun, both for me and the people who work here. You spend your whole life here. You can make it a prison, but I think it must be enjoyable.

DS: Your focus at Manco is really not a bottom-line focus.

JK: You can't focus on the bottom line. The bottom line is a result, not a cause. The numbers are phenomenal, but I don't get driven by numbers. I got a report today from a good guy in our department who did a study for us on expanding the building. If I used that report to expand the building, I would make every mistake in the book.

It's all wonderful stuff, but the fact is it doesn't account for the future, for your guts, for your belief in yourself, for how many other people you can sell that belief to. Now, I have to put all that to work. They call it guts. It's just a phenomenal belief in yourself that says put the damn thing out and build it twice or three times bigger. And don't worry about it. You can grow into the dream, and you justify the dream if you know your business. I guarantee you Wal-Mart didn't get big that way. I've read the book recently on Andrew Carnegie and great American entrepreneurs and not one of them got there by a set of numbers. They did it because they believed in themselves, and saw a vision of something bigger than anybody else saw, and they were busy building big enough buildings to house their dreams.

It's like Tom Peters, he's an MBA. He would like to shoot most of them. They are a bunch of number crunchers who never learn any human skills. Only two years ago Northwestern and Harvard (in fact, Northwestern just jumped way up and is the top business school) were first of all these so-called giant schools to teach courses in humanities and rope climbing. Where were they for thirty years when they were putting out drones or number crunchers who ran to Wall Street and created greed? I don't paint them all with the same brush, but when you're young and ambitious and you come through Harvard, which is one of the most competitive, intensely competitive schools, then you're primed to go to Wall Street. If you are the best of the best you get hired, but if you're not making $300,000 in two years you feel like you're a schmuck. So, now the cycle stops. You do whatever it takes. Ivan Boesky cheats, the kid cheats . . . welcome to the eighties.

DS: How is it going to change?

JK: It's changing right now. Banking systems are in disarray, politics are in disarray, lobbyists control politicians. A lot of things you can't change and can't control are now fixing themselves. The gong is going back this way. People are getting back to commonsense values of family, black-and-white basic issues. Drugs, I believe, are probably going downhill.

DS: What about this macho image, this addiction to logic?

JK: You need numbers, but I don't make decision from the numbers.

I get the best people, I create a good environment, and I try to get out of their way so they can do their jobs. I encourage them, try to learn to be part of it, and the profit is the end result that keeps getting better. You can't do it the opposite way.

Chapter Seventeen

Champions

> Example is not the main thing influencing others. It is the only thing.
>
> —Albert Schweitzer

Defensive, fearful behavior can sometimes contaminate entire groups. The wounded inner child acts out defensive and destructive behavior. It is like viewing a group of adults who appear to be overgrown kids who have not had their needs met. They can be belligerent, stubborn, and hostile. Sometimes it is masked in hurtful toxic humor. The behavior is so powerfully contaminating that the energy of an entire group is drained, and soon there is consensus—but this time it is negative consensus.

I have observed this behavior among people in a number of organizations. One of two things occurs. Enlightened leadership moves forward, empowering the positive, imprisoning the negative, and trusting that while change is slow, positive behavior will eventually be effective. It works. Such leaders are champions of change.

Unenlightened leaders do it differently. They stop moving forward in an effort to appease the naysayers and minimize the discomfort. This empowers the negative and defeats the positive.

It also works. The dark side, the Goliath, has been strengthened. Although this may appear very simplistic, our attitudes are the foundation of absolutely everything in life.

One group of managers blamed me for this kind of destructive behavior. Blame ("It must be your fault") is yet another form of defensive behavior and is quite abundant in our culture. This group finally broke through the denial and made painful strides in opening their communication about, and taking responsibility for, their behavior and feelings. Their apologies and requests for forgiveness were heartwarming as they shed another layer of barriers.

The media, particularly television and motion pictures, bombard us with images that the mind assimilates and interprets as reality. In fact, Professor Hazel Markus, at the University of Michigan Institute for Social Research, connects the media to possible selves in that we draw from a pool that we see around us.

Unfortunately, they often sweep us into a realm of behavior that is frequently violent, greedy, sexually oriented, and plastic. These models take us down the dark side path.

Thoughts emanating from our brain can either cure or kill our dreams of hope, or us. Seventy-five to ninety percent of illness is due to stress. Stress is reported to cause one thousand chemical and physical changes in our body and brain. There is evidence that stress kills brain cells, and that brains have probably been permanently damaged by stress chemicals from traumatic life events. Our thoughts and emotions affect our immune function. As a leader in corporate health care, Patricia Horvath brought Bright Side seminars to British Petroleum of America to weave together the concepts of mind, emotions, stress, health and performance. Her strategy with Bright Side was leading-edge.

Richard A. Lazarus, National Institute on Aging grantee, working at the University of California at Berkley, found that the frequency of the irritations of everyday life—traffic jams, cancelled appointments, tight schedules—as well as the uplifts, were more accurate predictors of psychological and physical health and morale than were major life events.

As I viewed the media and our lives, so many of which are stressful and unhealthy, I yearned to take positive images to people through one one of the most powerful weapons of our culture: television. Kim Shiller, an executive producer of "USA Today on TV," was young, bright, creative, and understanding of the inner child. Her own recovery and active participation in a twelve-step program fueled her desire to produce a Bright Side segment for her show. She wanted to provide tools of joy, love, hope, laughter—positive alternatives to the stressful, negative, garbage thinking that too often contaminates us.

I recall traveling to Manhattan to produce our first segment. As luck would have it, I wound up in a traffic jam in New York City. (What could be more stressful to my midwestern personality—than clogged New York traffic and me in an expensive BMW, stick shift no less.) I was tense. None of my Cleveland driving experiences had prepared me for this!

I even wondered if the Bright Side tools would work against some of the cynical and sophisticated New York attitudes. After all, this is the city where guns, shootings, and purse-snatchings are common daily experiences.

The tool of choice for the first Bright Side segment: bubbles. If bubbles work in Manhattan, they can work anywhere, I thought. And work they did! Taxi cab drivers, businessmen, the sophisticated and the unsophisticated, all concurred with laughter. Blowing bubbles helped them feel happier, more relaxed, and joyful.

On the bright side, I encountered on another New York trip a delightful taxi driver whom I shall never forget.

Returning from New Jersey en route to the Newark Airport following AT&T workshops, I rode with this chatty cab driver.

He was filled with joy and enthusiasm. He told me about his daytime job. He was a postman, and he talked about his customers as though they were his family. In fact, he referred to them as family. He told me that when people were on vacations, he made sure that their houses were safe, and that when he delivered packages, he would leave a note inside the mailbox as to where these packages could be found in some safe hiding place. I was fascinated hearing his stories. It was late at night and he had worked a full day as a postman walking from house to house, yet here he was, so alive, alert, and happy.

One time, he said, he delivered mail to a man, and upon arriving at the person's house he realized the man was not well. He called the emergency squad and had him taken to a nearby community hospital. He then told me that he followed up to see how this person was doing, calling the family and making sure that he was on his road to recovery.

He also told me about the living room deliveries that he made to an elderly couple who had difficulty moving around. He would bring the mail right into the house into whatever room they were. As I heard all these examples of how he delivers his mail and how he actually cares for people, I was amazed that he did so out of the goodness of his heart. Studies have shown that in the process of giving, we actually feel better. We influence the neuropeptide system of biochemicals and, in fact, cause our bodies to have elevated levels of endorphins, which are natural mood-elevating biochemicals. And that's exactly what I saw in this man. His mood was elevated. He sounded joyful and alert. In delivering mail he acted as though he was on commission, with each good deed increasing his income.

I believe that workers like this New Jersey postman really deserve to be honored, not only for the good job that they are doing but for the tremendous role modeling for customer service that they can provide. Let's look at higher standards and how to elevate them. The main way that we can elevate higher standards is by taking champion people and putting them in the presence of others. This cab driver was a champion performer, just as Allison Roe was a champion marathoner. There are champions in every industry who need to become the role models of today and tomorrow.

I'm reminded of that whenever I think of one Christmas. My friend and I were to have lunch together. She suggested an Italian restaurant, Massimo Da Milano, on the near west side of Cleveland. We were greeted by a parking valet attendant whose welcoming smile was an instant clue that I was going to have not just an Italian lunch—but a great Italian lunch. We were welcomed by Tony, the owner, who recognized my friend, much to her delight. The enormous restaurant was packed. I quickly checked out the food. It looked outstanding. I then knew lunch would be an adventure.

The scrumptious food was surpassed only by acts of warmth and kindness.

Tony sent over made-on-the-premises lemon ice and elegant Italian cookies. Then he sent us out the door with two loaves of homemade bread. Feeling treasured, we were once again greeted by the valet attendants who were interested in knowing exactly what we ate and how we liked it. With heightened enthusiasm, they described their favorite dishes. Parking attendants, who are usually considered minor players in the restaurant business, set the stage for caring, and reflected the same love, passion, and positive energy as Tony, the owner and their leader. My friend and I had a wonderful adventure because of the caring conveyed by the entire Massimo Da Milano team. For me, there has never been a more unforgettable dining experience. I yearn to return—all because of the standards set by one caring man who made me feel special.

This was in sharp contrast to an afternoon at a prestigious

shopping mall, when the valet attendant left me feeling ignored and passed by.

After returning from shopping and dining at this highly acclaimed center, I waited and waited for an attendant for service. Finally, after a ten-minute wait, I was told they could not find my keys. After much scrambling, the keys were found. It still took some time for me to get my car. The promise he gave me left my heart empty, "The next time you come, the parking is on us—and remember to come during hours I'm here." I have no desire to return. When will business discover that all contributions are important—and that the lasting ones often come from the first or last?

☆ *BRIGHT SIDE ENERGIZER* ☆

This is championship behavior I will take into action today.

____

____

____

Chapter Eighteen

Bubbling

> Thinking is the hardest work there is, which is probably the reason so few engage in it.
>
> —Henry Ford

> Risk with joy.
>
> —Donna Rae Smith

That precious kindergartner that lives within gets squashed as we grow up. Growing taller, bigger, and stronger suffocates the optimism, creativity, joy, and gentleness that is so abundant when we are five.

The garden God has made for us to grow in was wonderfully depicted in a painting I viewed at Progressive Insurance Company. It was colorful and looked as though it had been painted by the hands of a child. In the midst of this free-form painting were two childlike figures of Adam and Eve. I believe the garden inside all of us is to grow greener, more colorful, more loving and creative as we mature. Yet, how can we accomplish that with the child locked up so tightly inside us? This precious child becomes more and more distant by the constant taking on of guilt, shame, humiliation, fear, violence, power, and control.

As we grow up, we become more familiar with the tools of power rather than the tools of play. The simplest way to release your kindergartner is to pull out a childhood toy of joy. My favorite is soap bubbles. Everyone has had a great and positive experience blowing bubbles. Bubbles don't get confused with the competitive toys of childhood.

For example, I use toys in my seminars to help people break barriers, to reframe experiences, to lock in a positive experience and memory from the seminar, or to help people become comfortable with stretching, trisking, and trying new concepts. Because some people are uncomfortable with the concept of toys at work, I decided to experiment with the paddles and balls that are attached by rubber bands thinking those toys would be more masculine and accepted. A funny thing happened. Those paddles and balls didn't bring back great childhood memories of fun. They brought back memories of how difficult it is to use that toy. Few Bright Side participants were having success (or fun) with the paddle and balls. Most participants wanted to trade them in for soap bubbles or balls and jacks.

Another approach I have used is to allow seminar participants to select their toy-of-choice. Often the toy-of-choice is the bubbles. Simple. Splendid. Creative. Pure. Joyful. Bubbles.

So grab your bubbles and begin to activate your positive child self. Recall the games you played with bubbles as a child. Picture yourself blowing hundreds of bubbles or an absolutely huge bubble. As you bubble, recall more of the childhood joy of simplicity. Feel the oxygen cleanse your body with each bubble-blowing breath. Feel yourself become increasingly more relaxed as you breathe in goodness and breathe out tension.

Allow yourself to become more imaginative. What are the different ways you can blow bubbles? Can you develop a new way to blow bubbles? Can you blow a bubble inside a bubble? How about a bubble chain? Can you put your finger inside the bubble without breaking it? (Yes, but be sure your finger is thoroughly covered with bubble soap before inserting it inside the already blown bubble!) Incidentally, if you answered no, you need to play more in order to relax your mind and activate your right brain, the source of imagination. When we become judgmental, we stop the natural right brain–left brain flow. The left hemisphere is the source of logical, analytical thinking. The right hemisphere is the seat of creativity, intuition, and imagination. Our creative mind is vital because it is the source of new ideas. These are critical to professional or personal problem solving, inventions, and discoveries. Bubbling relaxes the mind and body. Relaxation is necessary for peak performance and health. It reconnects us to that tender, lovable, positive child that lives within us.

Let your tender child come out.

Picture yourself at age five blowing bubbles.

As you continue bubbling, begin to put positive emotions, ideas, and thoughts in those bubbles. Visualize your dreams and goals. Place those pictures of success in the bubble. If a negative idea catapults from your mind, stomp or break the bubble that is holding that idea. Begin to express feelings of love and liking of others inside your bubble. (Remember how important love and liking are to our sense of worth, to positive recognition, to trust or trustworthiness.) Express feelings of forgiveness for yourself and others to let go of barriers that hinder you or your success. As you blow bubbles allow yourself to go outside of the coloring lines, to fully experience freedom, acceptance, individuality.

Blowing bubbles certainly beats arguments, according to one Bright Side participant. She keeps her bubbles out on the kitchen counter. Frequently when things are tense in their household, the family blows bubbles to break the tension. Better than blowing hot air and regretting angry words, she explains.

One group of employees uses the office fan to blow bubbles, every Friday afternoon. It's a simple way to revitalize the team, get more energized at the end of the week, and to recall the positive experience of the Bright Side workshop.

Influenced by the bubbling, one of Bright Side's associates went out with three friends on a sunny afternoon with two bottles of bubbles. Needless to say, blowing bubbles in town brought laughter to them and to the bystanders. One man, in fact, tried a Bright Side suggestion: blowing bubbles in different ways. This one was walking backwards while trying to blow bubbles. Try as he did, he simply could not coordinate those two efforts. Recently, in a job interview, when he was asked about any personal experience he had that he couldn't do, he quickly remarked, "I can't walk backwards and blow bubbles at the same time." His skillful sense of humor broke the barrier of formality and endeared him to the prospective employer. He got the job. (No doubt he was bubbling positive images of success!)

The most touching example I have about bubbling comes from a mother who told me about her child. As a gift to my son and daughter, I present Bright Side programs to their classes. A full year following one of my school presentations, a mother came up to me to tell me that her daughter begins each morning by bubble blowing, filling those bubbles with positive affirmations about being lovable and awesome. Try it. Blow those bubbles and place inside each one loving, encouraging, affirming statements about your very own awesomeness.

Another group of managers broke barriers, cleansed their minds, and played with new visions of performance by blowing bubbles, forming clay objects, and then coloring pictures of their future organization. The whole intent was to become imaginative and to go outside of the lines and habits that had formed their current status.

When we pull out toys of childhood it helps us break out of doing things in the same way. It gives us a fresh perspective. Whether we are blowing bubbles, coloring, or hugging, it is almost impossible to be in conflict or in a state of mistrust. We are utterly pure and vulnerable, deeply aware of the wonderful childhood experiences of positive emotion and trust.

One executive keeps crayons on her desk to doodle new ideas and concepts.

Another group of managers was asked to partner with a team member in order to discuss their differences and what life event shaped them to be who they are today. They discovered more similarities than differences. Then they drew large pictures of each other as they each imagined the other to be as a young child. The very worst thing that could happen is that they would be wrong. Isn't that the excuse we give for not trying a new approach? Fear of being wrong. Yet, in a very playful manner, they built trust by trisking their own thoughts and by learning more about each other.

I have noticed that winning teams and winning athletes hug, kiss, and touch also. There have been studies that demonstrate that winners hug and get hugged more often. There was a study at Ohio State University that showed rabbits remained healthy, in spite of a high-fat diet, as a result of much petting and stroking.

Team spirit and human health are greatly enhanced by various approaches to hugs. In Bright Side seminars, coworkers are encouraged to appropriately hug each other, whether it is a huddle hug, a high-five, or a bear hug. Many of us are uncomfortable with such an open expression of touch because we have learned about touch in the wrong ways.

At Original Copy Centers, the "inner child" is released at the company's traditional Halloween parties. Great thought goes into creating Halloween costumes, even to the extent of making costumes that resemble Original Copy Center's product—black-and-white copies in sizes ranging from the traditional 8 1/2 x 11 paper up through all the other copy sizes that they provide.

At Forest City, the creative child was encouraged to experiment with new ideas. One way that message was disseminated was through a mailing of "fun packs."

For marketing budget meetings, Forest City sent out "fun packs." They wanted their marketing directors to look at mundane things they have to do for budget cutbacks—and look at them differently. Marketing directors came to budget meetings more open and ready for these reductions. They were eager to discuss new approaches to their challenges for 1991—which include standard items like how to get customers to shop.

Fun Pack: Balloon Helicopter
9 Color Pens
Mini-Puzzle
Runner's Cap
Chocolates
Squirt Gun

They came to view things in a different way. Reception to budget reductions was received positively because they had been approached positively year-long. They approached it from looking at the Bright Side.

Forest City employees also encourage and congratulate each other with letters that include stars and "Get Energized" stickers—a takeoff from their annual meeting when Bright Side "Get Energized" programs were offered each day during a three-day conference.

Or you may also want to try a pledge:

> I promise to keep myself energized. When I'm nonenergized, I'll use the stars, bubbles, my positive nickname, etc. I promise to help you stay energized. When I see you nonenergized, I'll give you stars, bubbles, or call you by your positive nickname.

If none of that works, try looking in the mirror, giving yourself a huge hug and then repeating the Bright Side "I am awesome" cheer.

I am awesome.
Yes! Yes! Yes!

or as one of the participants contributed,

Give me an **A**
WE
SO
ME

☆ *BRIGHT SIDE ENERGIZER* ☆

• *Bright Side Bubbling Meditation*

Take out your bottle of Bright Side Soap Bubbles. Begin playing with them, blowing big beautiful bubbles into the room, filling your room, filling the air with laughter, joy, love, and playfulness. As you blow these bubbles, remember your goodness. Remember your creativity. Remember how lovable you are. Enjoy your natural success mechanism. Enjoy your human instinct for health and healing. And as you do that, allow yourself to become much more relaxed and more playful.

Think of the games that you played with bubbles as a child, blowing the biggest bubble, blowing as many bubbles as you could into the sky, into the room, into the air. Blowing double bubbles, triple bubbles and breaking all of those bubbles before they reached the ground. Feel yourself becoming more relaxed, more creative, more playful, and certainly more optimistic. Fill your entire body, mind, and spirit with this uplifting mood of enthusiasm. Feel yourself becoming renewed, refreshed, and cleansed. Feel all of your cells responding to this enthusiasm.

As you feel your body becoming more enthusiastic, begin to relax even deeper. Breathe in very slowly, very comfortably, just like you did while you were blowing bubbles. Breathe in very slowly through your nose saying to yourself, there's nothing to bother me. Allow the oxygen to circulate throughout your body, cleansing and refreshing all of your cells. Blow the air out through your mouth saying to yourself: I feel calm and relaxed. And feel yourself becoming calmer, becoming more relaxed and refreshed. Gently close your eyes, concentrating on the slow, deep, easy breathing, the breathing patterns from when you were blowing bubbles. Blowing beautiful bubbles. See the rainbow colors in these bubbles. Picture one beautiful bubble surrounding you. This is a bubble of light. A bubble of love, protecting you, protecting your goodness, protecting your life, protecting your mind, your energy, your enthusiasm. Protecting your playfulness, your humor, and your laughter. Protecting all of that positive and creative power. All of those healthy and successful mechanisms within you. Feel and see this bubble of love and light completely surrounding you. That bubble is always with you.

And now, just as easily, form another bubble. Form it very easily as you slowly blow air into it. And now, empty out and remove from your body and your mind all of your negativity. Remove and empty out guilt, anger, pain, hurt. Empty out all of the barriers to your own happiness, to your own healing. Empty out the barriers to your own love, your own beauty, and your own success. Take the next thirty seconds to empty out negativity and tension and barriers.

And now that you've emptied out all of the negativity, send this bubble filled with negative thoughts and emotions far away until it becomes a tiny dot in the distance. Then pop that negative bubble! Explode it! It's gone!

And now, way in the distance, you can form another bubble. This is a bubble filled with positivity. Because this bubble is within your control slowly bring it back to you. This bubble of your Bright Side, filling you with love, happiness, joy, and the healing power of our Creator. Feel yourself filling with goodness and creativity, strength, peace, hope, forgiveness, and love. Feel all of that goodness. Feel that Bright Side filling you, becoming larger and brighter and greater. And moment by moment, feel yourself becoming happier, more confident and joyful. Moment by moment and day by day feel each positive thought, each positive belief. Expect goodness. Remember, that bubble is always with you. That bubble is for emptying out negativity and filling up with positivity, for emptying out the dark side, for filling with the Bright Side.

And so find a place to keep it. Anywhere in your body. A secure place. Now anchor it in that safe place. Anytime you need a mood lift, anytime you need to empty out negativity, anytime you need to be filled with your natural success, bring out that bubble and use it! And remember this bubble of goodness. Let it fill your Bright Side each and every moment of each and every day.

Chapter Nineteen

Managing Your Bright Side

An Interview with Mark Randol
President
Forest City Commercial Management, Inc.

One of my strengths is people strength.
—Mark Randol

Mark Randol joined Forest City in 1979 as president of the Commercial Management Company. He is responsible for over 16 million square feet of retail space located in shopping centers from the West Coast to the East Coast.

Forest City Enterprises, Inc., is a major national real estate company that develops and manages properties, shopping centers, office buildings, hotels, apartment complexes, and land. Of the top one hundred developers in the country, Commercial Property News in 1990 ranked Forest City second.

Forest City now owns more than $1 billion of completed properties at cost in its real estate portfolio. The company currently has more than $5 billion in projects in construction or development comprised of more than 22 million square feet.

The company owns and manages twenty-nine shopping centers (16 million square feet).

DS: What was the whole goal bringing Bright Side in? What did you want to accomplish?

MR: To start with, we looked at past seminars to see how we could improve them. People have heard me speak enough. It's always good to have somebody on the outside who will reinforce the things that you have said. People from the outside seem to have a better way of communicating this because they are not with the company. What they say is fine, but employees know it's not the boss and therefore do not have to take notes. They do not have to do anything the speaker says.

We did some research and brought Bright Side in, and, as you recall, we had three very good meetings. We all felt very comfortable with your abilities and talents and your methods of communicating with people. We have a great group of people, as you know. They're very open and very honest, and we thought they'd find some fun in all this, and they did.

DS: What apprehension did you foresee when we first started talking about the kinds of programs that Bright Side would do?

MR: I had some about gimmicks, like blowing bubbles, and balloons. Is this really for adult businessmen and women or is this for preschoolers? But this is the way you were able to bring out those feelings in the people. That's really just a small part of the program, but it was a way of breaking down barriers. There are usually some people out there who say, I'm not going to do that, but there wasn't a one. We took chances, but you must take chances. If you don't, you're not making a decision.

DS: And you want your people to take chances in some things. You want them to be risk-takers. That's part of the message.

MR: Absolutely. I do this all the time with them. I tell them where I see the pitfalls, but I let them go ahead and do it. The thing to do is not to be embarrassed about making a mistake, but to be smart enough to admit it and correct it. Sometimes, you try to correct the mistake and you make another mistake. No big deal.

Anyone who makes decisions is going to make mistakes. If

you don't make a decision, you're not going to make a mistake. I would rather have people out there making mistakes. I let them make decisions.

DS: Going back to how your people were touched, they were really into feelings and emotions. Why do you think that's important?

MR: First, I think it offers a sense of belonging. When you work for a large company, you feel you could be just a number. I never want anybody to feel that way.

It is very important for my people because they are all over the country. But it's very important for them to communicate with one another. I tell them to see our other shopping centers when they travel. They say, I thought my shopping center was nice, but this one is even nicer. And I belong to this great company that has nothing but wonderful real estate all over the country. I'm part of an organization that has these elements all over the country. And by communicating, they find that they are not alone.

DS: So really, what you're saying is that when you deal with this more personal aspect of a person, the emotions, he or she becomes a stronger individual and performs better.

MR: Yes. It manifests itself in the day-to-day tasks, and the job and especially their dealings with people, and that's really the business we're in. We're not in the business of running real estate—we're in the business of working with people. We are working with tenants, leasing personnel, maintenance personnel, supervisors, peers, and owners to accomplish a bottom line to the business.

So you have to develop very good people skills, and I think before you can do that, you have to like other people. But before you can like other people you have to like yourself. Sometimes we don't understand what really makes us tick, because we're always looking at somebody else. We never look at ourselves.

You gave the people the opportunity to look at themselves,

which was very important. That's where you really help break down the veneer, if you will. We all have a veneer. This is my business attire. I wear this only to do business. I wear this to play; I wear that to the gym. And it's all a facade. This is how I conduct myself when I'm with my personal friends at cocktail parties, and this is how I conduct myself at a board meeting, and this is how I conduct myself at other places. We develop trappings and skills that we think we have to use in order to get by. I don't think that is ever going to change, but just really trying to be yourself at all times is most important. You strive for that. You find that you don't have to wear all these different masks in different places.

DS: When people really know who they are and have confidence, they can be at peak performance. I was touched because it was a group of people who did in fact take off their masks. It was a beautiful experience for them as well as for me.

MR: We had a lot of new people, as you well know. Some of them had been with us say a day or two. Others have been with us for a long time. They were all looking forward to your meetings and waiting for you to come back.

DS: You had a very strong childhood, as I recall. You were given a lot of love as a little boy. I remember you sharing that with me. Do you think that has given you character today?

MR: Sure. You were talking about how we were all brought up with no's, but I don't think I heard that. Sure, I heard no. But it was never anything very strong. We had rules and regulations around the house, but for the most part, they were very simple, very broad, so we wouldn't be punished. Mother didn't like to punish, so she didn't give us very many no's. Because if she gave you a no, then she would have to follow through. After each spanking, my mother always made a point afterward. She said, this just kills me. She never did it in anger. It was very methodical. She said, "I told you if you did this, this is the punishment you're going to receive, and I have to follow through. And it just kills me to have to hurt my babies like this. But this is what I have to do. You are going to learn."

Afterward, she would hold us and kiss us and say, "I love you so much. You're my baby." You knew you hurt her, and you broke the rules, you received your punishment, but you always knew you were loved.

Each of my brothers and sisters has that same ability. We're all very successful professionally and socially. All of us have tons of friends. We still get along just beautifully. We still get together two times a year and everybody just gets along fine. A lot of the spouses love to come to the family reunions. They wouldn't miss them. And it's just amazing, how this large family just gets along so well! No fighting, bickering, jealousies that you would typically have in some large families. Mother never liked that type of thing and there was never any cause for them. She was never a gossip, never talked about anybody. She never talked about friends. We were not brought up with any of that around. It's only when we got to the outside that we found that people would talk about their closest friends as soon as they walked away.

DS: During the session, you said that the kind of love that was so abundant in your life was lacking in many of the people who work for you.

MR: I found that with most everybody, not only the people I work with. I found that I was brought up so differently. There is a long story behind it.

My mother was an only child, and she came from a fairly wealthy Texas family. She was sent off to boarding schools all of her life. She just absolutely hated them. She had every material thing she ever wanted, but all she wanted was a brother or a sister. But her mother would not have any more children because she had been the oldest of eighteen children, and she had to perform a lot of the chores as a young girl. She wasn't about to do any of that again. She didn't even want to have the one child. So my mother said when she got married, she would just have tons and tons of children. She had nine children who lived to maturity, two children who died before the age of two, and a couple of miscarriages. She went to her grave saying the only thing she regretted in life was not having more children.

DS: How beautiful. Your mother must have been very close to God.

MR: Almost too close! She was a very good woman with high morals and ethics, and she bestowed that on all of us. Her children were her whole life. She took us places, on vacations. She was always there with us.

DS: Do you remember during our session, I asked everybody to recall a love experience? Did you talk about something from your childhood in regard to your mom?

MR: Mother was Mother. She was a great woman, but she never smothered us. There were never any demands made upon your time. She would invite my wife and me over for Thanksgiving after we married. She'd say, "If you can come, fine, if you can't, I'll understand. Don't worry about it." She never wanted to be a burden. After my father passed away, she refused to move out of the big house. We said, "This is more house than you need." She said, "I love this house. I have servants who will take care of me. We'll live here and everything will be fine." We said, "What if anybody breaks in?" She said, "Who is going to break in? I'm a seventy-five-year-old woman." She did not want to move in with anybody. None of us children have an obsession with my mother's love as nurturing. It was just so matter of fact. It is only when you get older that you find that it was something special.

DS: Do you see yourself nurturing your people?

MR: Oh, yes. I love people. I love kids. That is the first thing

I do when I interview. If I don't like them, then I don't hire them. If I don't like them, I figure nobody else can.

DS: How do you keep a positive environment here with everybody so spread out?

MR: Telephone calls, personal visits to the shopping center, inviting them to the home office for meetings, budget reviews and the like. We have a monthly newsletter for employees, with all news about them, who's doing what, where, or special events. It's a way of getting their name in front of everybody else and pumping them up. If they're pumped up, automatically I'm pumped up.

DS: You have very much a "can do" attitude. How do you instill that in other people?

MR: When we have openings of shopping centers, I bring a team of people in, the managers and market directors who run the company, to work on a similar project. Two weeks prior to the opening of a shopping center, we do everything to get the shopping center ready for the opening. Each person is given assignments, something challenging but not overwhelming. Before you know it, as each day goes on and as the big day gets closer, they see where it's going. We're going to make it.

DS: I have talked to a few of your people about using Bright Side ideas and tools, and I was really very pleased to find out they have been taken into action at the shopping center level, as well as here at the corporate level. What ideas have you specifically taken from the sessions?

MR: It wasn't necessary for me to do much. My people here have learned so much that they are getting psyched up. Their attitudes toward others in the office, some of the barriers have broken down, and they discover that the person next to them, who may be a competitor, is still somebody they like and respect. Petty bickering has lessened.

We do things here in the home office which we have been

doing for quite a while. Like on Valentine's Day or Easter, Halloween, any occasion, we'll have a lunch and have a "dress down" day where they can wear whatever they want to. Everyone brings food and they share recipes and really get into it.

DS: That's a very good idea. I want to go back to what you said just a couple of minutes ago. After the sessions, you noticed less bickering among your people and more openness, respectfulness, and caring and liking. Do you have a specific example that comes to mind?

MR: Some of the secretaries say, "That's my job and that's your job." I try to say, "You're all responsible for everything." I want everybody to share and help the other person out. That's easier said than done. Certainly, there are people who will always pitch in. Others would see that and they would start working, and they were satisfied when they saw they could help.

DS: So you really are seeing people give more?

MR: Yes, giving of themselves, which is more important than anything else. Giving of their own time and their own efforts.

DS: So there is increased morale, more individual esteem and worthiness. That also means increased productivity.

MR: Right.

DS: That is wonderful. Are you surprised?

MR: Yes. We didn't think that that was why we were bringing you in, but that was one of the benefits that came out of it.

DS: What other benefits have you or the company received?

MR: Managers now talk to each other, go see each other. They would only do that on a very limited basis before. I have noticed there are also more telephone communications and personal visits. A lot of times people arrive at the sessions and sit right next to somebody from California. They talk with them, but they still don't know them. That's why I have planned socials every night during the annual management meetings.

The reason for the social is for people to get to know each other personally. What you did for us in the meeting portion was to expand upon the socials. Our people really got to know one another and themselves, which is something they do not do in my socials. The sessions allowed people to take off their masks and be real with one another, finding they had more in common than they thought.

DS: I know you are a unique individual. Do you think that your kinds of values, thinking, and philosophy are abundant in our whole American working environment?

MR: No. It's unfortunate, but I'm a realist. I'm not ashamed to say that I think I'm bright and smart and good, and I do a lot of good things. But I think one of my strengths is people strength. I like people. If you like people, you are just generally nice to them, and you're caring. You want to see them grow. You want to help them. You don't want to do anything to hurt them. That is not a learned quality. It's something I think you are just born with.

DS: What I find very interesting is that it does influence productivity. How do you think that message can be conveyed to more people who are in such a competitive global market? How would you suggest other leaders try to do what you're doing?

MR: As I said before, it's just liking people. I remember when I first came to the company, they told me they thought I was probably going to have to replace most of the managers because they didn't think they had the qualities to run the business. I told them I'm not the type who comes in and sweeps everyone out. I said I wanted to give the people out there the opportunity; to let them know what the challenges are; what work has to be accomplished; and give them the time, tools, and money to do it. I have only one manager who transferred to advertising and marketing with us. Everybody else who was with the company eleven years ago when I started is still with me today.

DS: So why were they able to perform better under your leadership?

MR: I gave them challenges. I showed them what had to be done and set standards of excellence. I empowered them to lead. Good people, when they're trained, can be accountable and responsible. They can get a shopping center cranking out the dollars.

All the employees take pride in working for a company that is strong and healthy. They take pride in the tenants, the customers, and the physical appearance of the shopping center. The customers and tenants are constantly stroking the managers, telling them how beautiful the shopping center is and how wonderful the promotions are. Therefore, the managers can't slip. Their families come in and are impressed. They take pride in it. This creates ownership and loyalty.

DS: In other words, unlike your predecessor, you set high standards, and you conveyed to your people that you believed they could do it?

MR: I knew they could do it. It's that positive attitude. I believed in them and they began to believe in themselves. The company was amazed that I was able to keep the people. My confidence in them probably activated already existing seeds of confidence planted in them in their youth. The managers in the field completely turned around and really became bright, smart businessmen, knowing everything about their properties. There is nobody here doing their work for them. They are doing it all themselves.

DS: It sounds like there was mediocrity under another form of leadership.

MR: Well, it wasn't mediocrity. It was just that the person who had my position before had really never been in the shopping center business or perhaps squelched the manager's belief in self.

DS: I think a lot of times companies do think they have to get rid of what they have in order to be really excellent, but you said these people want to do a good job, so you're going to show them how to do a good job and create the kind of environment so that they can do that.

MR: You give them the tools. If you bring somebody in from the outside, you still have to train them, motivate them, and make them understand what you want. So why not give the person you already have, who has loyalty to the company, why not give him or her the opportunity?

DS: Do your people have even better relationships with the tenants today than they had a year ago as a result of what they've learned in the past few months?

MR: Yes. Managers must have strong relationships with the tenants so the tenants understand that we are there to help them through their problems. We want to keep them happy, not just stay with us.

DS: Do you have any examples?

MR: When I first came with the company, I got tons of phone calls from tenants. I told them to call the manager responsible. I told the managers to address the problem and they did.

DS: How challenging is your industry right now?

MR: It is challenging primarily from the standpoint of new development. The insurance companies and the banking business have been stuck with a lot of bad real estate. We have a good reputation in the business, and the money is not as easy to come by as it was before, but we still have a strong track record and banks are willing to make us loans.

DS: What makes you number one?

MR: I think there are a lot of things. I think one is our locations within the marketplace. Also, the design of our properties is very good, but that's a very small segment. More important is the selection of merchandise and the tenants that we bring to our customers.

We try to give the customers a good blend of merchandise. Now, they can go to other malls to find similar merchandise. We give them the most diverse selection and a clean and safe environment to shop in. We have good hours, special events, and customer service centers. We take care of the shopper's personal needs and to try to give each of the shopping centers a feeling that someone is there who cares. In most malls, there's nobody there. It's just a huge building with a lot of stores. The place has no personality, no heart and no soul.

DS: I love this idea that you just mentioned a moment ago, the heart and soul, and that's developed by your people. Really, what you have been developing is the heart and soul of your people, and it comes across in the whole shopping center environment. That's wonderful. How are you going to continue change and growth, learning?

MR: One of the things we just started this past year is a cart program, where we have vendors on push carts in our centers.

If you have two shopping centers in the same market area, you are competing for the same customer. If it's fifteen minutes to this shopping center and fifteen minutes to the other one, why would you pick mine over the one down the street? All the merchandise is the same. So what's going to cause that shopper to pick me over the other? If I can develop an atmosphere in a shopping center, and you walked in and you saw these beautiful push carts, with great lighting, beautiful, well-displayed merchandise, you just get excited. There is such an uplifting feeling when you walk in!

I want to tell people, you're here to shop. It is going to be so much fun, you're going to have the best time you've ever had. We are going to offer you a beautiful broad selection of fun, different, unique merchandise that cannot be found anyplace else. When you see it on a cart, it says "temporary" and you better buy today because it may not be here tomorrow.

DS: Fun and uplifting is really what you are talking about. Making it fun, kind of like Disneyland and Disney World. When you go to places like this it's such a wonderful, fabulous feeling. You feel good about yourself.

MR: As you know, shopping is one of the first things that people look to for entertainment. So, how much better can the merchandise be? To walk into a shopping center that has all these carts, you don't know if you're going to make it to the other end of the mall because you're having so much fun going from cart to cart, store to store.

DS: Are there other areas you would like to explore or expand in in terms of having fun, being uplifting, and being entertaining?

MR: I have always had this concept that all shopping centers look like an architectural wonder, with beautiful skylights and big fountains and large landscaped areas, big open spaces, places for entertainment. I want to see a shopping center look like the biggest department store you ever walked into.

Instead of having storefronts, you would have little showcases out front, with merchandise just like the department stores. Down the middle of the shopping center, you would have handbags, belts, accessories, perfume, jewelry, and lamps on the counters. Everything would be very low in the middle of the kiosks.

When the consumer went in, she'd know she was here to shop. This is a real shopping center, not just a large space designed by an architect but an environment to sell this cup and saucer. We're not selling fountains and birds and trees. We're selling merchandise. Give the architect the challenge and have him build me something where I can sell this teapot, suit, or dress.

DS: You want to create a pattern or a habit, a positive one, uplifting one, and you want them to buy lots and lots of merchandise. That's what it is?

MR: I want to make certain that we have the merchandise the customers want, and give them a pleasing environment and services and amenities, that the shopping is a true fun experience.

DS: What would you say to other leaders who really need to change in this highly competitive market?

MR: As I said before, you must like the people who work for you. I only bring anybody from the outside when my people have turned down a position. I promote from within. And I work very closely with all of my people in developing their careers, what they want to do in life. Where do they want to live? What shopping center do they want to handle, and do they want to move there? It's not important that they move. There are some companies that if you don't move, then you're passed over, and if you don't take it, you're gone. I don't do any of that. I just say, where you are now, I need you. But I want to satisfy you. If you think that there's someplace you want to go, I'll send you there to take a look at the community. If there's something you think you want to do, it's there for you. If not, I'm going to be just as delighted that you're staying where you are.

It's my job to find somebody for that center. That's not their responsibility. That's my responsibility. I want someone who, moving to Manhattan, Kansas, is elated with Manhattan, Kansas. Otherwise, productivity goes down, interest is low, and the person not happy.

DS: What words of advice would you give to other leaders?

MR: We all have the same needs, whether we are the boss or not. We all want to be treated with respect and dignity. We all want autonomy, the ability to make decisions on our own and suffer the consequences. And all of us want to be financially rewarded for what we do. Praise doesn't put food on the table. Employees have to be rewarded financially.

They also need to be nurtured and have somebody who will listen to them. Each of us makes an important contribution to the company. If he or she doesn't feel important, then all of it is for naught. It can't be superficial.

DS: Do your people need to come to you if they have an idea and they want to put it into action?

MR: For the most part, yes. If it's changing procedures or policies or changing physical appearances and real estate, yes. Beyond that, there are so many things that are out there that they can do on their own.

DS: Earlier, you had mentioned the apprehension about the balloons, the bubbles and the stars and the Awesome stickers. Now that you have experienced them, what do you have to say?

MR: They were great! They were perfect. They were simple enough so people understood what they meant. It was like being a kid again. It let us bring in the positive as opposed to the negative.

DS: When we recall things that are negative, it is very imprisoning. When we recall things that are positive, it is extraordinarily empowering. I think that the tools help people remember what they experienced and learned. There is also something that they can take back and use.

MR: These people pass out stickers on different correspondence. They put a little sticker on it, and they remember the meeting.

DS: You really treat your people as treasures.

MR: I treat them the way I would want to be treated. It's those small things that you do that become very important to them.

DS: There probably are a lot of leaders who do not bring together the personal with the business, the emotional with the rational. What would you like to say to them about the value of doing that?

MR: All of us spend more time at the workplace than we do with our families. That's unfortunate, but it's a reality, and that's not going to change. Therefore, your business environment is, in reality, an extended family. None of us really wants to think that we depend upon our office relationships for living, but if you are not happy there, it's going to be very difficult to be happy at home. The emotions and feelings are always with you. So, you should try to take the environment where you spend the majority of your life and make that as meaningful, fruitful, and happy as you can.

But you have to create an environment. You can't just ban bickering and gossiping. You must create an environment where these things do not occur and let everybody know that everybody is working on the same team, no matter if they're in different departments. All of us are working towards the same goal. It's up to each of us to help the person next to us to do his or her job.

I try to develop a team within the organization. I would rather have people talking and getting to know the person who sits next to them. I have no strict rules about breaks. The only thing that I ask is that there is always somebody to answer the phones. There's free coffee. We have a kitchen, so people can bring their lunch from home. When you strip all of it down, you're spending more time here than you are at home. Why not have the work environment be an extension of your home?

DS: A lot of Americans, because of the way they were taught, repress their emotions and do not take them to work. What do you have to say to that?

MR: I think emotions have to be felt and expressed. Otherwise, it leads to mental anguish and frustration. How do you express emotions at work? I think expressing anger is healthy, although in the work environment it must be expressed appropriately. Actually, I want to give people very few occasions to have to express that type of anger. Anger really comes from frustration. When you are frustrated, it means that you can't accomplish the task, or somebody else couldn't do what he or she was supposed to do to get the task accomplished.

DS: There is a tremendous amount of mistrust in today's environment and in the world. Do you think that your organization has greater levels of trust than most other organizations?

MR: I can't speak for other organizations. I know throughout the industry we put more trust and responsibilities on our people in the field. They are responsible for administering the expenses of about two million dollars per property, and they go through the bidding process of the contracts. They review people, hire people in the field, do the maintenance work and repair work in the shopping center. They know they are trusted with a multimillion-dollar property. They know they are responsible for it. They are given rewards and bonuses based on the results. They have an incentive to do well, to be honest, and to take that trust and responsibility seriously, and they do.

Chapter Twenty

Love

> The best and most beautiful things in the world cannot be seen or even touched. They must be felt with the heart.
>
> —Helen Keller

> There is no meaning to life except the meaning man gives to his life by the unfolding of his powers.
>
> —Erich Fromm

After moving to Cleveland, one of my first acquaintances in broadcasting was Jane Temple. Jane, now married with three children, had decided to leave her prestigious position at the local ABC-TV affiliate to spend more time with her family. She and I had arranged a meeting to review broadcasting projects.

I looked forward to seeing her. When Jane arrived at my office, I immediately learned that this past year, at forty, she had had open-heart surgery. Stunned and feeling vulnerable, I questioned her as to how the surgery had changed her life or her outlook.

Jane was open to sharing her heartfelt emotions, her own mortality, her childhood experiences. She had a family history of heart ailments and resultant early deaths. For the first time in our twenty-year friendship, she shared little-known aspects of her personal history.

Jane had seen her own mother die at an early age because of heart problems. Jane was raised by her aunt and uncle. I could picture Jane, as a teenager, being cared for by this couple. However, she then shared with me that her relatives raised her from the time she was a very small child because her mother had never fully recovered from her divorce. Jane's revelation of herself, her identity, and her feelings created a bond of trust that I had never before experienced with her. I felt safe.

"Jane," I asked softly, "did you know my sister Debby died of cancer this past year?" We looked directly at one another in mutual understanding of loss, protected by this new armor of trust. I realized that our friendship was very rapidly deepening. In a few brief minutes we built greater confidence and strengthened our relationship. Although we had maintained a loose friendship over a period of years, we were never emotionally intimate.

The trust that is so necessary to positive relationships sprang out of her honest expression of her own vulnerability. Through trust and openness I had discovered the real Jane. She was authentic, not the image I thought she was, or the image our media and culture painted of her identity. I trusted her authenticity not because it was perfection but because it was truth.

This bridge of truth gave me the courage to talk about my sister's death.

Debby had breast cancer that metastasized throughout her body. It was a very devastating and painful condition. Debby was a holy and extraordinary woman who thought about the welfare and happiness of others, not lamenting or feeling sorry for herself in the midst of her excruciating pain. I remember how she empathized with my son's diabetic condition, being sensitive to his daily blood tests and injections and the mood swings sometimes incurred in high blood sugar levels.

Her sweetness and childlike qualities were shared with my son. She told him she understood his suffering because of what she was experiencing in the hospital with cancer. My son stopped to hear her more carefully, completely touched by her compassion and sensitivity to his condition, and overwhelmed because he knew her cancerous condition caused excruciating pain far exceeding any discomfort he had experienced.

Debby knew how to love, even in the midst of cancer. Her love knew no boundaries as she was able to reach the deep inner spirit of every life she touched. It was through simplicity, truth, love that she enriched others' lives—not through exterior images of power or control. Her experiences of loving others released a flood of heartfelt emotion and a deep bond of trust. Actions of love create trust, relationships, and loyalty.

The same model, when applied to corporate environments, creates the model of excellence required for productive, caring team members and quality service. First, team members experience deep caring, emotion, and love from leadership and associates. This in turn creates enthusiasm, loyalty, and commitment for industry goals of service excellence and customer caring.

"Jane," I said, "Debby knew how to love." During the last two weeks of her life, she was quickly approaching a deep sleep. She spent much of her day with her eyes closed, yet fully conscious of her surroundings. One late afternoon, sitting next to her hospital bed, I told Debby that I knew she loved me.

"Debby," I said, "I now know you love me, that I can trust you . . . simply by the way you look at me." Without hesitation, Debby opened her eyes, wide and bright, and looked deeply, intently, and for a very long time directly into mine. Her look was so deep, loving, intense, and lasting that the intimacy was almost uncomfortable.

It created a new self-awareness—for me to understand how conditioned we are to accept less love, little or no intimacy, and to pretend that the sexy images presented in media are love and intimacy. I knew Debby's gift and look of love took great physical effort. She gave to me the greatest present of all—the gift of love.

"I know exactly what you mean. I was at WEWS-TV when Dorothy Fuldheim had her stroke," Jane said.

Dorothy Fuldheim was a Cleveland legend. A pioneer in broadcasting, highly opinionated and controversial, Dorothy broadcast live interviews and commentaries daily until the age of ninety. After a stroke at age ninety-three, she went into a coma. Jane was asked to organize a celebration for Dorothy's birthday. The station executives, who were not only Dorothy's employers, but also her friends and support group, wanted to bring Dorothy a birthday cake.

Jane remembers Dorothy being in the coma, apparently unaware of birthday well-wishers. Jane sat next to Dorothy and said, "Dorothy, we love you." Dorothy opened her eyes, looked directly at Jane, and said, "I hope so." Their deep inner core of love and spirit touched each other. Even for Dorothy Fuldheim, the beloved broadcaster, the most important thing at her life's end was to be loved.

As Jane related this to me, both of us were crying freely.

Do we have to wait for life's end to discover that we are loved by others, and that we have loved others? The famous Dorothy and the simple and holy Debby, at the close of their physical lives, were concerned most about the lasting meaning of their lives. That lasting meaning was love. One was to be loved. The other was to give love.

Since I have shared this experience with thousands of people, I have come to realize that this deep need for love as described in those two women's lives is universal.

"Your every act should be done with love" (I Corinthians 16:14). But what is love? Is it that sensuous image thrown at us from television, music, movies? No, the best definition of love is from the New Testament.

> Love is gentle, love is patient, love is kind. Love is not jealous, it does not put on airs, it is not snobbish. Love is

> never rude, it is not self-seeking, it is not prone to anger; neither does it brood over injuries. Love does not rejoice in what is wrong but rejoices with the truth. It always protects, always trusts, always hopes, always perseveres. Love never fails.
>
> I Corinthians 13:4–8

Since love is so vital to all people everywhere, how is it that we have such difficulty understanding, living, and interpreting it? The barriers to love are as universal as the need to love and be loved.

I was entertained by a clown mime who depicted the life of a person from birth through adulthood. At first, the girl-clown-mime was filled with joy as she began experiencing the wonders of life. Like the Ashly Montagu film of a toddler exploring his world with energy and wonder, this mime reenacted a child's freedom, enthusiasm, spontaneity, and exuberance. The pantomime was thrilling to behold as the child freely formed abundant hearts of love which she gave away in total honesty and openness. The sense of freedom, love, and hope grabbed my heart.

As the pantomime continued, the girl-clown-mime began to sense rejection. Her love was not being accepted. She became stiff, uncertain, insecure. The hearts she had once shared so abundantly and freely were now smaller, fewer. The exuberance, confidence, and love were fading. I noticed that love was being blocked by masks or barriers.

The first mask I recognized was one of hurt, followed by masks of anger, then belligerence. As the child grew older, a mask of rebellion was added. She added promiscuity, alcoholism, drug addiction, materialism, self-pity, and violence, until she could no longer survive under the weight of her burdens.

Her true self, expressed in her ability to give and receive love, had been totally crushed as she took on the negative feedback she frequently heard which strangled her self-esteem. Eventually, it choked her spirit.

In the pantomime, the woman, in her darkness of despair, discovered the source of love. In that inner experience, she was saved. She experienced love and felt hope. It became the source of her courage, empowering her to strip away the masks. With resistance and difficulty, one by one, she removed the masks of destruction and the barriers to love. She began loving . . . but there were still masks creating an invisible barrier. Now the only masks left were the masks she really enjoyed. What masks do we cling to that ultimately stunt and block our growth, our ability to love, our individual creative energy?

For the mime to love, she had to let go of destructive, limiting masks and habits—even the ones which she liked and admired.

Once we let go of these barriers, negative habits, and masks, we can love unconditionally and freely. As the mime finished her performance, she exuberantly formed the huge hearts of love, breaking thorugh the invisible wall she had once hidden behind.

Love. We all want it. Why wait till death to ask for it, to acknowledge its importance and to give it? And how can we bring love, caring, and respect into our work environment?

The individual is the most precious resource of corporate America. When machine tools are properly maintained and remanufactured, they produce quality products. So do people. When properly cared about, individuals produce creative and quality ideas, attitudes, and actions. What determines the performance of either resource is the inner essence, not the glitz. Remembering the "Good Samaritan" story, people are more likely to be kind, to give, to serve, to be helpful when they have been treated in the same way. Acts of power will never produce acts of love.

How do we bring love into work? Certainly not by looking deep into someone's eyes and telling them, "I love you."

For the moment, let's imagine that love and respect are the same. When I visited the manufacturing facilities of Nakamura-Tome in Kanazawa, Japan, I read a book about Japanese home factories. The concept intrigued me, particularly when I read about embroidery crafts and traditions that were perpetuated by master craftsmen in a home factory in Kanazawa. I contacted the hotel information center, requesting information about a tour.

"Would it be possible," I inquired, "to view the home factory specializing in embroidery?" After a long delay, I was told yes. Since it had taken so long to get a response, I again inquired if it was appropriate to make such a tour? "Yes, Yes, Yes." I was once again reassured.

Some moments later, a taxi arrived: it took me far out into the countryside of Kanazawa. Excited by finally arriving, I did not question the distance. The cab driver left.

I went up to the home in the country, quite different from the life-styles I had observed in the cities such as Tokyo and Kanazawa. I was greeted by a warm, friendly smiling face. "Hello," I said. The woman bowed and responded in Japanese. I realized that she spoke no English.

She led me to the second floor of her home, a bright clean, simple room filled with women sitting on the floor embroidering over very low tabels. I saw magnificent works of art, created with gold, silk, linen, silver threads. The embroidery was so intricate that it appeared to be a majestic tapestry or painting.

I was then greeted by the master craftsman, the man who owned the home, knew the craft, and ran the home business. He spoke no English either. Everyone smiled at me. Still no English from them—and no Japanese from me. I wondered how we would communicate.

The I heard the doorbell ring and footsteps coming from the stairs. In English, a Japanese man introduced himself to me. He explained that he was brought in as an interpreter from the local university in Kanazawa. How amazing and gracious of them, I thought, to bring in an interpreter just for me, one single human, one American! I felt very respected, very special, and very valuable.

I am, by nature, curious. Through the interpreter I inquired about the beauty of the craft. Then I requested something that I later learned was totally outrageous. I wondered if I could have a wall hanging embroidered of these magnificent gold, silk, silver, and linen threads. I heard "Yes, Yes, Yes." Arrangements were made for its delivery. When I left, I felt like the most significant person in the world. I couldn't wait to return home and hang this masterpiece in my living room.

I radiated excitement when I returned to the hotel. It was then that I learned the outrageousness of my request. The purpose of the embroidery factory was to embroider the *obis* of ceremonial Japanese kimonos. The wall hanging that had been so graciously planned for me broke every Japanese tradition and custom as the embroidery technique, dating hundreds of years, was for the exclusive purpose of adorning the cummberbunds for the Japanese traditions which required ceremonial kimonos. The Japanese did so much to treat me with respect. I felt respected, valued, *and* loved.

I learned the lesson of the YES Attitude in Caring and how it generates feelings of love. It certainly was many levels above the sterile American policy of service ("It isn't my fault," "I can't do anything about it," etc.) because it treated me as a valued individual. The depth of the embroidery factory experience matches the unconditional love I experienced from my sister.

Remember the Good Samaritan effect: that we all want to be loved. First we must love one another, then love our team members, our clients. By treating each other as our best client, as the most important person in the world, as though God has sent us to serve one another, we can have a better world and be a model of service excellence that is admired and duplicated by others.

I had an excellent American service experience while traveling the East Coast. I had finished three days of presentations in Washington, D.C., and was traveling to New York City. True to form, I was close to take-off time when I arrived at the airport. One skycap must have noticed how I scurried, for he announced that he would give me service like I had never had before.

As I mentioned earlier, I am a curious person. I mused, what could this service be like? As time was very precious, I did not have the luxury to ask him. Rather, I said that I would appreciate that kind of service. With a huge smile, he grabbed my briefcase and garment bag and asked for my ticket. He whisked me to the check-in counter and checked me in. Then he suggested that I follow him. He bubbled with enthusiasm. He walked me directly to my gate. Yes! Yes! That was service like I have never had before. That became my American caring model for service, and it was reminiscent of the service I had enjoyed in Japan.

Please take a moment to think about an experience you had in being respected, cared for, valued, and loved. Allow yourself to relax and bring to mind this past positive. You may choose a very intimate experience similar to the one I had with my sister. You may choose an experience more closely aligned with the Japanese embroidery factory, or the skycap at the Washington airport.

As you recall this caring model, bring to mind where you were, what happened, and how you felt. Allow yourself to fully experience the feelings of love and respect. Begin to also picture a past positive experience where you did something similar for another, giving him or her love and respect, know that what you did brought that person lasting feelings of goodness, respect, love, and worth.

Let those *past experiences* become your models for caring. Share verbally those experiences and take them into action with a minimum of three people in the next twenty-four hours, encouraging others to share similar past experiences. Allow those past positives to help you establish new standards and perspectives in love and service. Notice that the memories that you bring to mind will probably be simple kinds of opportunities that we often overlook or deem insignificant.

Pat Cassese, the CEO of Antares Group, told me that his organization had grown so large that he seldom had the opportunity to go onto job sites and talk to his employees. But one night, when he went to a job location, one of his first employees, overjoyed by seeing him there, gave him a hug and told him how happy they all were to have him there!

Pat had forgotten how important his presence was to his team; yet the underlying and deeper significance only became apparent as he shared his caring model with other CEO's. It gave him a deeper sense of his personal value, causing him to feel loved by his employees. He experienced a meaningful work relationship that he almost skipped over, that he now wanted to bring home and share with his wife. CEOs, like everyone else, have the same need to be loved, valued, and appreciated.

THE GIFT OF LOVE

One day not long ago, I received a most precious gift. A person who had attended early Bright Side sessions stopped by to tell me he purchased a business. He looked happy and confident. Then he confided how I had helped change his life.

He said he couldn't agree with all my principles, yet I was the person he turned to over one year ago when he was in the midst of destruction, because he knew he could trust me. Knowing his chemical addictions were destroying him, he had placed his life in my hands. He felt his life was hopeless and out of control.

I walked with him in this time of genuine pain and loneliness, introducing him to a twelve-step program and taking him to Mass with me. I was able to openly share what I knew and travel with him on this new path of hope and self-discovery. His visit was to thank me for this precious relationship and to celebrate his new beginning.

Neither power nor money could have ever purchased this precious gift of life and relationship that we both received . . . a deep richness in meaning, heart, and spirit.

☆ *BRIGHT SIDE ENERGIZERS* ☆

- Recall feeling loved anytime in your life.
- Fully experience feeling lovable just the way you are.
- Develop a strategy to give your coworkers or clients an exciting and caring moment of service.
- This is what gives meaning to my life.

____

____

____

Chapter Twenty-one

The Transformer—The Gardener

In his mind a man plans his course, but the Lord directs his steps.

Proverbs 16:9

I had had lunch many times at a restaurant in Cleveland called The Greenhouse. One particular afternoon, I was having lunch with the school superintendent. I looked above my head and noticed strikingly beautiful colored stained glass, apparently from a church. It was the first time that I noticed a stained-glass window in the ceiling even though I had eaten in this restaurant frequently.

As I looked around, I noticed that there were many stained-glass windows around that I never had seen before. In the one directly overhead, I saw a colored reflection of two men. Who were they, I wondered? The only thought that came to my consciousness was Jesus and Peter, his disciple. Without thinking about it much further, I continued my lunch.

That evening I thought again about never having noticed those beautiful windows in the restaurant. I wondered if the two men really were Jesus and Peter. The reason for the significance was that the previous Sunday at church, our Gospel was from John

21. In it, Jesus had appeared for the third time to the apostles. The apostles were not far from shore fishing. Jesus, from the shore, gave them instructions on what to do with their net. When they followed his directions, they caught so many fish they thought that perhaps their net would break. It was John who recognized Jesus. Upon hearing that it was the Lord, Peter threw off his clothes, jumped into the water and swam to shore. When he got to shore, he had a conversation with Jesus. The Lord asked him, do you love me more than these? Peter said, you know that I love you. Jesus told him, "Feed my sheep."

As I began to contemplate that Gospel, I thought how much it fit with a book I had finished reading, the autobiography of Bishop Fulton Sheen. In that book, the only Gospel that was elaborated was the story from John 21. That evening, believing that the stained-glass window at The Greenhouse restaurant was also Jesus and Peter, I felt excitement mount. I saw how these pieces were coming together. I had attended church and heard the reading of John 21 about Jesus and Peter. I had finished an autobiography of Bishop Fulton Sheen, where that very same Gospel was discussed in length. Lastly, at lunch, in the restaurant, right above my head, was a stained-glass window depicting that same scene. Within a matter of several days, three very closely related ideas and events merged. All I needed to do was confirm that the restaurant's stained-glass window did depict Jesus and Peter.

I picked up the telephone and called the restaurant. I spoke to the manager, whom I knew well. She confirmed that those two men were indeed Jesus and Peter. She also said that when she was in church that past weekend, the service was based on the same Gospel. That was solid confirmation for me. All the pieces were coming together in the same way that colored glass comes together in a magnificent church window.

How often do we overlook those circumstances where the

pieces come perfectly together and match. In fact, if we were to describe this to others, they might laugh. Yet this is how we know our prayers are answered. We know that our prayers are answered by confirmation, physical and emotional signs that show us we are following God's plan. And the only way that we are aware of this happening is by connecting to that Higher Power deep within ourselves. God will give us the circumstances and the people we need in order to fulfill His purpose, and to fulfill our desires and needs.

How many times do we miss the messages that are intended for us because our eyes are not wide open, because we are not in prayer, because we are not tapped into our spiritual selves? How many messages do we miss because we are out of the current of spirituality?

To me each day is a triumphant day, an awesome day. Each day has very specific messages for us to help us utilize our talent and abilities. And each one of us brings to the whole big tapestry our experiences, our expertise, our knowledge, and our talents. But our color in the tapestry only becomes brilliant and clear when we are listening to the will of our Higher Power.

We talk so often in the corporate sense about creating team spirit and encouraging people spiritually. In order for people to develop spiritually, they need to have the freedom and encouragement to listen to and trust their inner sense. And that inner sense goes beyond man's philosophy and man's principle. It is a quiet spiritual sense. We can only have successful teams and successful companies as we allow people to be completely and totally successful in all elements of their lives: the physical, the mental, the emotional, and the spiritual.

As I look back on the experience that I had in The Greenhouse, I know that that was an absolutely perfect environment—the picture of the greenhouse that we all live in—this great wonderful world where we need to be encouraged to garden our creativity and our creative talents. The gardener of this great wonderful world is our Higher Power, God, and each of us is here to do something to make it a better place. We each have our own set of tools and talents for gardening our mind, heart, and spirit and the heart and spirit of our greater community.

I wonder what we are doing in the corporate world to feed, nurture, and tend to God's people. What are we doing to help people utilize their potential, tap into their talent, and feel filled with love, joy, and purpose? So often, I look at the working environment and I see the opposite happening. People are filled with stress, anxiety, tension, and fear. They have no sense of purpose other than the bottom line and helping a few people greedily put huge sums of money into their pockets.

That is why I think that Nancy Vetrone at Original Copy Centers, even though she has never used the words ''God'' or ''spirituality,'' is feeding and tending God's sheep in the way I believe God intended. Nancy is looking for ways to care for people to help them grow. Not only the people within her whole organization, but the people within the community.

She is a very powerful example of how a crisis transforms our lives. As CEOs of companies, it is our responsibility to utilize our lives in a way that produces fruit, not only for ourselves but for others. It is gardening the garden that God has given us, the garden that God has begun and still tends. As in the case of Nancy Vetrone, she used a negative experience in her life to produce a harvest for many other people, to give others opportunities for fully living and loving.

Some time ago, I was asked to present a Bright Side series of programs to a group of CEOs. It was a very exciting opportunity for me because it was for presidents and CEOs from the industrial Midwest. It was fun because the day for my first presentation was February 14th—Valentine's Day! When I think of Valentine's Day, I think of trust, love, emotion. And of course, the symbol is a heart. This first CEO presentation on Valentine's Day was in a building called Genesis. In my mind, Genesis is creation, God's creative work.

Love and work—two vital ingredients for all people. Work gives a sense of meaning, using our talent to fulfill our own purpose and to take creative action, which requires courage. Love is a sense of being cherished and treasured. What I would like to suggest is that in our work environment we develop more ways for people to use their abilities, to fulfill their purpose so they will have greater joy and belonging, feeling like a precious treasure, a tended sheep. That is feeding and nurturing God's sheep.

☆ *BRIGHT SIDE ENERGIZER* ☆

- Pray or meditate on a proverb or psalm. Here are a few for you to consider.

> For God has not given us a spirit of fear, but of power, and of love and of a sound mind.
>
> 2 Timothy 1:7

> Let us not grow tired of doing good, for in due time we shall reap our harvest, if we do not give up.
>
> Galatians 6:9

> But they that hope in the Lord will renew their strength; they will soar as with eagles' wings . . .
>
> Isaiah 40:31

Chapter Twenty-two

Living Happily Ever After

Most people are about as happy as they make up their minds to be.

—Abraham Lincoln

I received this gift in today's mail . . . from a NASA employee who keeps Bright Side going with this wonderful idea of a "Certificate of the Right to Play," written by Bruce Williamson.

Certificate of the Right to Play

By this certificate know ye that

____

is a lifetime member in good standing in
The Society of Childlike Persons
and is hereby and forever entitled to

walk in the rain, jump in mud puddles, collect rainbows, small flowers, blow bubbles, stop along the way, build sandcastles, watch the moon and stars come out, say hello to everyone, go barefoot, go on adventures, sing in the shower, have a merry heart, read children's books, act silly, take bubble baths, get new sneakers, hold hands and hug and kiss, dance, fly kites, laugh and cry for the health of it, wander around, feel scared, feel sad, feel mad, feel happy, give up worry and guilt and shame, stay innocent, say yes, say no, say the magic words, ask lots of questions, ride bicycles, draw and paint, see things differently, fall down and get up again, talk with animals, look at the sky, trust the universe, stay up late, climb trees, take naps, do nothing, daydream, play with toys, play under the covers, have pillow fights, learn new stuff, get excited about everything, be a clown, listen to music, find out how things work, make up new rules, tell stories, save the world, make new friends with the other kids on the block, and do anything else that brings more happiness, celebration, relaxation, communication, health, love, joy, creativity, pleasure, abundance, grace, self-esteem, courage, balance, spontaneity, passion, beauty, peace, and life energy to the above named member and to the other humans and beings on this planet.

Further, the above named member is hereby officially authorized to frequent amusement parks, beaches, meadows, mountaintops, swimming pools, forests, playgrounds, picnic areas, summer camps, birthday parties, circuses, cookie shops, ice cream parlors, theaters, aquariums, zoos, museums, planetariums, toy stores, festivals, and other places where children of all ages come to play, and is encouraged to always remember the motto of The Society of Childlike Persons:

IT'S NEVER TOO LATE TO HAVE A HAPPY CHILDHOOD
BEGIN TODAY!

☆ *BRIGHT SIDE ENERGIZER* ☆

This is how I am going to play today.

____

____

____

Appendix

Other Bright Side Energizers

If men and women practiced mental calisthenics as they do physical calisthenics, they would purge their brains of worry and stress.

—Arnold Bennett

☆ *Bright Side Energizer 1* ☆

THIS BUBBLE IS FOR A NEW AND BRIGHT IDEA AS IT COMES BUBBLING OUT OF MY MIND!

____

____

____

> Do not follow where the path may lead. Go instead, where there is no path and leave a trail.
>
> Anonymous

☆ *Bright Side Energizer 2* ☆

After you finish blowing bubbles, make drawings of the bubbles filled with positive images, ideas, thoughts, and pictures.

You can eliminate negative thoughts in your bubbles by breaking the bubbles with your hands, causing them to disappear. You can break negative thoughts in your mind by mentally erasing them.

> If I could have one wish I'd ask all the birds to sing their best; all the flowers to bloom to their sweetest just for you on this special day.
>
> Anonymous

☆ *Bright Side Energizer 3* ☆

THIS IS WHAT I ESPECIALLY LIKE ABOUT MYSELF

Reach high, for stars lie hidden in your soul. Dream deep for every dream precedes the goal.

—Pamela Vaull Starr

☆ *Bright Side Energizer 4* ☆

THIS IS A NEW BRIGHT SIDE HABIT—TO REPLACE A NEGATIVE PATTERN OR ADDICTIVE THOUGHT

Things do not change, we change.

—Henry David Thoreau

☆ *Bright Side Energizer 5* ☆

THIS IS A POWERFULLY POSITIVE AND JOYFUL FEELING FOR ME TO MEDITATE ON

____

____

____

All our actions take their hue from the complexion of the heart, as landscapes their variety from light.

—Frances Bacon

☆ *Bright Side Energizer 6* ☆

HERE IS A RIGHT AND POSITIVE SOLUTION FOR ME!

____

____

____

Faith is the bird that feels the light when the dawn is still dark.

—Sir Rabindranath Tagore

☆ *Bright Side Energizer 7* ☆

GOTTA EMPTY OUT THE DARK SIDE

(Take away its significance by
making it small and faint)

When it gets dark enough, you can see the stars.

—Lee Salk

☆ *Bright Side Energizer 8* ☆

THIS IS A NEW AND BRIGHT IDEA FOR A SITUATION/RELATIONSHIP

I wish you all possible good and happiness.

—Beethoven

☆ *Bright Side Energizer 9* ☆

THIS IS A BRIGHT WISH FOR THE WORLD

____

____

____

Where there is no vision, the people perish.

Proverbs 29:18

Bright Side®

P.O. Box 284
Chagrin Falls, OH 44022
(216) 247-2611